When Faith > Fear ...

CARLY FREELS

WESTBOW
PRESS®
A DIVISION OF THOMAS NELSON
& ZONDERVAN

WestBow Press books may be ordered through booksellers or by contacting:

WestBow Press
A Division of Thomas Nelson & Zondervan
1663 Liberty Drive
Bloomington, IN 47403
www.westbowpress.com
1 (866) 928-1240

ISBN: 978-1-5127-1985-7 (sc)
ISBN: 978-1-5127-1986-4 (hc)
ISBN: 978-1-5127-1984-0 (e)

Library of Congress Control Number: 2015918991

Print information available on the last page.

WestBow Press rev. date: 11/30/2015

Contents

Foreword

Faith
... is a spiritual rebellion against the world's status quo.
... is the opposite of fear.
... is the confidence that Jesus is present and eager to collaborate with us.
... is something we do; it represents actions we take because of what we believe.
... is the supernatural capacity to see a bright future, even though the present looks bleak.
... is the God-given ability to hold on through the worst and to wait for God's best.
... is the conviction that despair is presumptuous.
... is inner assurance that the worst things aren't the last things, that God has the last word.

Faith may be hard to define, but we all recognize it when we see it. The Chinese proverb is correct: "One picture is worth ten thousand words."

The story of Carly Freels' hand-to-hand battle with cancer is faith's *Exhibit A*. Her testimony, unveiled in these pages, paints a beautiful picture of how to exercise mountain-moving faith. As Carly's pastor, I saw up close how she walked through diagnosis and treatment. Faith rose within her, and as a result, she became whole in ways previously unknown to her. Not only has Carly been healed of cancer, but she has been transfigured by the Holy Spirit from a garden-variety Christian teenager to a dynamic apprentice of the Lord Jesus Christ. It has been a beautiful thing to behold.

When a person stands on faith that the Almighty cares and "nothing is impossible for God" (Luke 1:37 NIV), look out; miracles happen. Jesus promised, "If you have faith as small as a mustard seed, you can say to this mountain, 'Move from here to there,' and it will move. Nothing will be impossible for you'" (Matthew 17:20). People who take Jesus at his word and act accordingly always experience transformation.

Some wise person said that everyone is either coming out of trouble, in trouble, or heading into trouble. Job observed, "People are born for trouble as surely as sparks fly upward" (Job 5:7). Jesus agreed when he said, "In this world you will have trouble" (John 16:33). No one gets out of this world without his or her share of difficulties, hardships, and pain. The thing that separates us is how we handle these trials when they arrive. It is Carly's hope that this book will elicit faith within the readers when trouble knocks at their doors.

Dr. Jim Jackson,
Former Senior Pastor, Chapelwood United Methodist Church
Author, *Covenant Friendship: An Ex-Loner's Guide to Authentic Friendship*
Houston, Texas

Preface

I am writing this book to provide a source of hope to all those coping with the effects of cancer. During my own battle, I turned to various books to gain knowledge on the subject or to provide clarity on how I was supposed to handle my diagnosis. However, I found that many books published on this topic were written with a negative dialect; they end in tragedy or lack any mention of faith. Reading these books failed to make my process any easier or shed any light on how my family, friends, and I should go about handling my newly-diagnosed disease.

One of my favorite sayings is, "Faith does not make things easy, but it will make them possible." If you get nothing else out of this book, I pray that you can see the only way to defeat something as out of your control as cancer is to rely fully on the Lord and have faith in the miracles that he is capable of.

To give an even deeper and more honest look into this time in my life, I have included the entries from the journal I kept during my diagnosis and treatment.

I tell you the truth, if you have faith and don't doubt, you can do things like this and so much more. You can even say to this mountain, 'May you be lifted up and thrown into the sea' and it will happen. You can pray for anything, and if you have faith, you will receive it.
—Matthew 21: 21-22 NIV

Dedicated in loving memory of Coach Tina Young
1966-2014
4CY

Chapter 1

Six-Letter Curse Word

Isn't it crazy how six simple letters can completely alter the path of your life? C-A-N-C-E-R. Those six unassuming letters suddenly take on the connotation of a curse word so that people feel the need to whisper any time it is mentioned in a sentence. "Did you hear she has *cancer?*" or "She's battling *cancer*" are sentences murmured in hushed tones with fearful faces, like a secret.

Nothing was wrong with me—I was sure of it. I felt fine; I looked fine; I was fine. There had to be a mix-up in the test results ... there just had to be. I read the doctor's lips as he spoke that life-changing, groundbreaking six-letter word, but I refused to believe it. A screeching ring took over my consciousness as the room faded to black, and my eyes wilted closed. Uncertain of how long I was unconscious, I was awakened by my mother's whimper and my father gently gripping my hand.

"You have Hodgkin's lymphoma," the doctor reminded me when I woke back up. "You will need to start treatments as soon as possible; however, the good news is *if* you are going to have a cancer, this is the one you want."

My thoughts swarmed at that comment; what was that supposed to mean? Who would ever *want* any cancer? Other six-letter words began to flood my head as Dr. Johnson continued to explain the procedure that we were to follow to restore my health—words such as *doubts, failed, finish.* Doubts about my future and what was to come of it. Failed exam results. Finish—finish was the hardest for me to grasp. I was finished with my volleyball career—finished with any dream of being recruited to play at a collegiate level, finished with my summers of a carefree two weeks at camp, and finished with a normal high school life.

Despite the uncertainty and confusion that came with this day, I was certain of one fact. This situation, this place in my life, was much greater than I was ever intended to handle on my own. If I knew one thing, it was that without God on my side, I could never win this battle. I promised right then and there, sitting on the paper-covered table, that I would not lose my faith during this trial. I would use this worldly disease to turn a test into my testimony. The Lord promises in Jeremiah 30:17 that he "will restore you to health and heal your wounds," and those were words I was willing to stand by—no matter what the hardship.

Journal Entry
April 30, 2012

I went in to get the test results today from last week's biopsy but everything is kind of a blur. Once I heard the word cancer, I didn't hear much after that. I went very light-headed for a while and began to hear only high-pitched ringing as I watched the doctor's lips continue to move—until the room went black. I didn't process any of what he was telling me after that. My mom was fanning me as she cried, and my dad was holding my hand tightly.

Even though hours have passed since the diagnosis, I am still in shock. I just don't know how to handle this. I do know that God is holding on tight and would never put an obstacle in my path that I couldn't overcome. I trust completely that there is a purpose for my having cancer, and although I don't know what it is yet, I promise to remain faithful to Christ throughout the trials and stand firm in my beliefs. I will pray that God will use this trial to show me the miracles he is capable of and heal me quickly and completely.

One of the things I am most afraid of is that people will start treating me differently at school. I don't want to miss out on my high school life and lose the normalcy of being a junior girl. Whether they pity me or become afraid to talk to me, I am just scared to see how everything is about to change. I guess this process will show me who my true friends are.

For I know the plans I have for you, declares the Lord; plans to prosper you and not to harm you, plans to give you hope and a future. Then you will call on me, and I will listen to you.
—Jeremiah 29:11–12 NIV

Chapter 2

Outsider—Day One

Hoping that I could enjoy a few more normal days, I had only told a few of my closest friends about my diagnosis, not yet becoming the girl who cued the whispers and uneasy stares. However, I had momentarily forgotten the capability of high school girls to take any piece of gossip and spread it school-wide in the blink of an eye. Every passing in the hallway was accompanied by a glance of empathy, a hushed comment to a friend, or an occasional dodge of eye contact. It was official—word had spread. Classmates who had always been "too cool" to start up a conversation with me were suddenly dying to know how I was holding up. They would flock to me in the halls, as if we were the best of friends, questioning in a dragged-out tone, "How are you doing?" You know the tone I mean, right? With the head tilted, slowly nodding.

"I'm fine! How are you?" always seemed to be my overly peppy answer for how I actually felt. Fine. I could have told you in all honesty that morning that I was in fact *fine*. It wasn't until I was drowned by helpless stares that I felt as if I too should be grieving. "Fine" became a word I used much too often those next few weeks.

I am the kind of person who never likes to admit struggle or defeat in my own life, so you can imagine that something as out of my control as cancer was not my topic of choice. I so badly craved to find my friends and talk about something other than the draining discussion of my well-being. It wasn't even first period, yet I was already overwhelmed with questions I didn't care to answer.

Finally, a glimpse of hope at the end of the hall—my four best friends were walking my way. They would know exactly how to handle this situation. They would understand that I wouldn't want to talk about anything health-related and comfort me with small talk of what everyone's dress looked like for the upcoming dance, how annoying our history teacher was, or what we would be working on in volleyball practice that afternoon.

As they approached, something seemed off. The normal excitement of seeing each other every morning was absent. The yells from down the hall were silent. Although we had acknowledged our presence from across the way, they walked right past me, as if I were suddenly an outsider in my own group. Not a word was said in response to my once again overly chipper, "Morning, guys!"

Silence. They continued talking among themselves as they strutted right by me, as if I were a complete stranger, invisible in their eyes. Were they done with me? Just like that? Because I would be out of volleyball until I was cured, did I no longer serve a purpose to them?

My thoughts were jolted by the high-pitched buzz of the morning bell. Shaken up, I wandered my way to physics class. As I walked in, I immediately noticed a stressed aura in the room as everyone flipped through flashcards and rustled for pencils in their bags.

"Everyone, be seated to start the exam," Mr. Waverly called from behind his desk.

In all the chaos of the previous night, I had completely forgotten about my physics test and was not at all prepared to take it. I contemplated my options. Option 1): Be like every other kid and accept that, ready or not, there was an exam today, and I had to take it. Option 2): Explain my circumstances and ask for an extra day to prepare. (However, he was the "no excuse good enough" kind of teacher, so there was a possibility of being turned down.) Option 3): He still had not seen me walk in, so it was possible that I could skip class today and e-mail him an apology for my absence, qualifying for a makeup exam. All I had wanted was for today to be another normal day, just like every other, and to be treated like any other student. It would be hypocritical of me to pick and choose how I wanted to be treated based on the benefits. For this reason, I decided it best to take the exam unprepared.

> Question 1: A biker accelerates uniformly from rest to a speed of 7.10 m/s over a distance of 35.4 m. Determine the acceleration of the bike.

I read and reread this problem, but I couldn't seem to shake my own problems from my head. Why were my closest friends ignoring me? Weren't they supposed to be my comfort in times like this? Why was I diagnosed with cancer? Was God punishing me? What had I done wrong? What would my coaches say? When would all of this be over? My mind raced much faster than any hypothetical biker in a stupid physics problem.

Hushed murmurs from the front of the room distracted me from the uneasy thoughts swarming around in my mind. I looked up and was instantly relieved at the person I saw. Ms. Christie was my math teacher from last year, who also happened to be a very close family friend; she was at the front of the room talking to Mr. Waverly and pointing in my direction. I was saved. She headed toward the door and nodded for me to approach the front of the classroom.

"I'm sorry, Carly. Hand me your test, and *you* tell *me* when you are ready to try again," Mr. Waverly assured me with another one of those looks of pity I had received countless times that day. "Ms. Christie would like to talk to you; you may be excused to go with her."

Ms. Christie was my favorite teacher as well as the mom of one of my closest friends, Katherine. No matter what it was, she was a consistent source of help with anything I needed, whether it was tutoring in math, advice on a problem, or a paper I forgot to print out the night before; Ms. Christie was able and willing to help.

"I figured you needed saving out of that exam," she said in the first genuine voice I had heard all day.

"I have a surprise for you in my room that is much more important than that test was anyway." As the door to her room swung open, a familiar embrace instantly took me in.

"Katherine! When did you get into town?" I cheerfully questioned. Although three years older than I, Katherine was one of my closest friends; she was currently a student at Baylor University.

She explained that she had heard about my diagnosis and came to see me. Finally—a response I'd hoped to receive from a friend. She said she knew me well enough to know that I wouldn't want to be pampered or flooded with care, but if there was anything I needed, she would be there in a heartbeat. Hand in hand, she slid me a stack of notecards bound together by a ring. Displayed on these cards were Bible verses about strength, healing, and hardships.

"Read these when you're feeling up to it," Katherine instructed. "Even when I am not here, I hope you know that these verses can comfort you and be a source of truth in suffering."

Meanwhile, I had overheard a few brief mentions of my name during a phone conversation Ms. Christie was having in the background.

"Carly," she suggested, "Coach Young would like to speak with you in the locker room. When you are finished with her, you are more than welcome to hang out in my room the rest of the day if you aren't feeling up to attending your classes."

I headed toward the locker room, pondering all that Coach Young endured through her own battle. I reflected back to that day two years ago when confusion and anticipation swept across every girl's face in the gym as the freshman volleyball team rallied together. Coach Young had just called for a team meeting to conclude that day's practice, and rumor had it that she had some big news to deliver. I can honestly say the message I had expected was not even close to the words that began to echo through my eardrums.

"I have Stage IV lung cancer," she began. "Ten months ago, the doctors told me I had six months left, but I have been blessed. I don't want to worry you with this news; I just want you to be aware of the situation. My doctors have recommended that I slow down my lifestyle and quit coming to practices, but that is simply not an option. You—my team, my closest friends—are the source of my strength, and your support will see me through this battle."

I remember my shock as I tried to make sense of what she had said. I could barely comprehend how someone who displayed such strength and fearlessness on the court could be dealing with such a terrible disease in her personal life. Maintaining her commitment to our team and exhibiting no signs of the struggles she must have been facing, I was in awe that she silently had dealt with this terrifying trial over the last six months. As freshman year progressed, Coach Young continued to amaze and influence me with her constant determination. Observing her consistent drive to beat the odds of cancer drove me to become not only a better athlete but a better person.

I had no idea I would soon be at a place in my life when I would have to revisit Coach Young's impact on my character. I had the impression it might start and stop with my freshman volleyball season; however, life has a strange way of recycling its lessons. I had a feeling that as I started my own battle, Coach Young would come to symbolize a new brand of role model for me in a way I never could have imagined.

I pulled back the locker room door, revealing a concerned Coach Young sitting at the table in the middle of the room, envelope in hand.

"Hey there, Chipmunk," she began in the most restful voice I had ever heard from her. Always projecting to make up for her small stature, she was one of the more high-energy coaches on staff. Coach Young had called me *Chipmunk* since day one of freshman tryouts. Before getting to know her, I took this name as a way to tease me and wondered if she even knew my real name. However, as time passed through the seasons and our relationship grew, I realized it was a term of endearment. And although she hated to admit it, I constantly teased her about how I knew I was one of her favorites.

"Have a seat. I want to chat, if you don't mind." I chose a seat a few down from the coach, slowly settling into it, preparing my mind to take in all she was about to say.

"I know I am not the most serious or emotional of people; we have that in common. But I want you to know that I know what you are going through. I have been there, and I want to be there for you every step of the way. I was diagnosed three years ago and always wondered why my battle with cancer was being dragged out so long when little improvement was shown; however, I think I found my answer. Part of my purpose in life is being brought to clarity today. I am here to help guide you through this scary journey you are about to begin. Any and all questions you have, come to me."

Coach Young paused and looked at me for a moment to make sure I was actually listening to what she was telling me. Although paying attention, I couldn't quite build up the courage to look at her while she spoke. Hearing someone tell me that she believed the purpose of being challenged with this earthly plague for so many years was to help me battle against the same thing was too much to comprehend.

"I will leave my talk at that, because if you are anything like I was the day after being diagnosed, you don't want to discuss it. I wrote you the rest of my thoughts in this letter; please read it when you are feeling up to it. No rush. Lastly, it is normally an extensive process to get admission into MD Anderson; however, I contacted my doctors and got you in for an appointment today. It's nothing to get worked up over; today will be easy. All you should expect is to meet your team and discuss treatment options. Your parents wanted me to tell you they are picking you up in the front office at 1:00 p.m. to meet your doctors. You are in the best hands there, Carly."

I remained still as I repeated the third piece of big news I had received in the last twenty-four hours. First: Surprise, you have cancer. Second: You are no longer relevant to your group of friends. Third and latest news: You do not have any time to come to terms with your diagnosis; you are going to the hospital in less than three hours.

Thanking Coach Young for all her time and concern, I began to wander back to Ms. Christie's room. I probably should have said something more to her about how much it meant to me that she reached out or asked her some of the millions of questions that flooded my mind, but it was all just too sudden.

Letter from Coach Young
May 1, 2012

Dear Chipmunk,

If you are anything like me, you are telling yourself everything is fine with your health and that today is just an average day, like any other. I know for a fact that you are just like me in thinking this, because I have watched you on the court for three years now. When you are struggling, you refuse to come out of the game because you know you can beat the slump you are in. When you get hurt or need a break to breathe, you never admit it; you simply play through it.

I have no doubt that you will do exactly the same with your diagnosis. You will beat the slump and continue to play through it. But at the same time, I want you to know you don't have to put on that "Don't worry about me; I don't know the meaning of the word defeat" look I've seen so often from you. I want to be there for you to offer pieces of advice when you're going through treatments. Things such as: when you get nauseous, eat ginger; when you are administered the red chemo, gargle salt water to prevent mouth ulcers; and don't eat your favorite foods during treatment, because there's a chance of them coming back up a few minutes later, and from then on, you can't stand the taste of them.

This won't be an easy fight, Carly, but with the support I know you have and the faith you have always stood by, there's no doubt in my mind you will come out victorious. The secret is to let people help you. You are not the only one this diagnosis is affecting; so let those who are suffering vicariously feel better about the situation by doing something to help you. You are not weak for accepting help, I promise you. Having said that, there will also be people who were in your circle before who simply will not know how to handle all of this and who will possibly make you feel forgotten in your hardest hour. Don't think of this as a loss. Thank the stars above for those who stick by you and really show up when they know you need them. Those are the friends for you—not the ones who vanished in fear of saying the wrong things.

I am going to try to start scheduling my treatments the same days as yours so that you will have a familiar face in the hospital. But I encourage you to reach out to other patients you meet at MD Anderson. Your constant smile will serve as a sign of hope to the kids you will be surrounded by in pediatrics, and a healthy-looking young woman like you, radiating confidence in a place of sickness, could alter a child's outlook.

I believe there is a reason for you suddenly having to cope with cancer, and I hope you can have faith in that reason, even if you cannot see it now. You are going to change lives through this, Carly.

Stay strong. Live without fear,

CY

Chapter 3

God's Hands and Feet

The second I stepped foot out of the car, I realized something about the sea of people flooding in and out of MD Anderson. Cancer doesn't discriminate. People of all walks of life were entering this building. Male, female, rich, poor, and every color under the sun—they were all fighting for their lives against this worldwide plague we call cancer. A sweet lady, Bertha, opened the car door for us and politely welcomed us. We walked through the main lobby, and I began to notice the 3 B's Coach Young had joked about. In overwhelming quantities, you would see Bibles, blankets, and bald people. She had mentioned that everywhere you looked you'd see someone seeking spiritual guidance, a scalp shining from the side effects of the chemo, or someone bundled in a blanket to prevent shivering from the cold air on their hairless heads.

Floor 6—the lymphoma and leukemia pediatric center. This was it. We wandered in and approached the front desk, unsure of what to do, yet trying not to look as lost as we felt. Patients' drawings and thank you notes decorated the room; inspirational quotes were plastered on every wall. There were TVs, toys, books, and video games covering every square inch of the space, providing distractions for every child's interests. I was easily the *elder* among the patients. I was still seventeen years young and therefore qualified to be a part of the pediatric center; however, it was hard to sit there and watch infants and toddlers suffering when they lacked the understanding of what they were actually enduring. It was obvious I was the new girl in town by my lengthy locks of hair I was desperately dreading to lose.

Michelle, the bubbly receptionist, eagerly smiled as she welcomed our family to MD Anderson. "I am going to put this wristband on you with your medical record number and birthdate on it. Doctors will require you to recite both of these before administering any treatment, so it is in your best interest to go ahead and memorize your record number. Have a seat with your family while you wait for Tony to call you back, okay, sweetie?"

Sweetie? It was clear that Michelle called all her younger patients by this name to make them feel nurtured, and it had become a word of habit, regardless of the patient's age.

I found a place to rest between my parents and two girls playing with their Barbie dolls. They were clearly sisters, as they resembled each other in every way except the length of their hair. While neither one of them could have been over the age of eight, one had a mane of luscious golden-blonde locks; the other featured a hairless scalp shaded by a Disney princess ball cap. Although the healthy sister seemed to trail in age, she seemed to take on a protective, older sister role. I'm sure this was a result of having to assist her parents in nursing her older sister back to health.

Texts had been flooding my phone all day with messages about people praying for me or wanting updates on how I was holding up. The only thing was, not one of these came from the numbers of those I used to call my best friends. Upperclassmen, parents, even teachers were all dedicating a second out of their day to wish me well—something it seemed my teammates didn't find important. Right then and there, I decided to stop throwing myself this pity party and realize that God had a purpose and a plan. The people he was calling on to reach out to me on a day of adversity were being placed back in my life for a reason. In the same way, there was a reason the Lord was removing certain people from my life. Just like Coach Young had mentioned, there will be people who will not be able to handle the pressure of seeing someone as a cancer patient. I needed to surround myself with the peers the Lord was guiding me back to, those who would be a positive influence in my life and who would challenge me daily to remain faithful.

"Carly? Head on back!" I heard a booming voice shout from the unseen. Seeing my confusion, Michelle gently smiled at me and pointed toward the back room. "That's Tony," she suggested. "She will do your blood work. Get ready though; she has a loud personality."

I walked back to the room that the loud voice was carrying from and had a seat in the chair being motioned to me.

"Well, hello there, young lady! Aren't you a tall drink of water! Pleasant surprise to have someone walk through my door older than the age of ten! Hopefully you won't cry and scream as much as they do when I draw your blood."

Every word Tony was saying sounded as if she were yelling to someone sitting back in the waiting room. "Have you had your blood drawn before?" she loudly questioned.

"No ma'am, but I hope I have the tolerance to handle it better than your younger patients. It would be embarrassing if I couldn't," I said, nervously laughing.

The truth was I hated needles, and even the thought of having blood drawn made me queasy.

"You will be fine, baby! As long as you had a big breakfast this morning you shouldn't feel nauseous at all, and this will be over before you know it."

Uh-oh. I had yet to eat anything that day, given all the nerves and chaos of my morning. I could feel this situation heading south quickly. I couldn't help but watch as she drew blood from my arm, vial by vial. It was like a bad wreck; you cringe to see it happening, but you can't convince yourself to look away.

"You don't look well, baby! Let me get you a wet rag. Don't stand up. I will be right back."

Her initial sense of excitement turned into a tone of urgency as she ran from the room to get me help. How embarrassing. She had consciously brought up the fact that I would be able to handle needles better than some other patients, yet here I was, seeing stars on the walls and fighting to hold my head straight on my shoulders.

"You'll get used to this, baby! We have to do it with each visit, so unless you have scans and are instructed otherwise, make sure you eat something before coming in. Sit here as long as you need to, and when you're feeling ready, head next door to see Alice."

Alice and Tony couldn't have been more opposite. While Tony loudly projected everything she said and used her large personality to make her presence known, Alice was a quiet soul. When I walked dizzily into her room, I barely noticed her petite figure sitting over in the corner. Whereas Tony's room was decorated as if it were a crime to show any inch of white wall, Alice simply displayed one lone picture taped up on the back wall. Her room was completely bare except for a poster of a small white Maltese puppy.

"Good morning," Alice nearly whispered in her timid Asian accent. "Please have a seat, and I will take your blood pressure and temperature."

I could tell I already liked this person as she slowly paced around the room. Although I am sure she performed the exact routine hundreds of times a day, she seemed almost uncertain of every move she made. Lastly, and without a word, she motioned for me to come over to the scale for height and weight. With a soft smile, Alice handed me my printed-out schedule for the day and showed me back to the waiting room.

"Enjoy," she murmured, turning back around to return to her white-walled cave.

"How did it go? What did you do? Who was back there? Did everything go okay?"

The second I sat back down, rapid fire questions poured from my parents. Once again, "It was fine" was all that I felt like explaining. Knowing my mother, I thought she would consume herself in worry if I mentioned that I almost passed out with Tony or would give me topics of conversations I should have had with Alice.

We were now back to just waiting. Sitting and waiting, making small talk to distract ourselves from the reason we were there and ignoring all the unknowns of what we were getting ourselves into. My mom sat directly to my left, frantically jotting down every question she wanted to ask my doctor when we met her. I subtly peered over the notes she was writing, making sure not to be caught for fear she would want to discuss every thought she had. My mom's page read:

Questions for the doctor:

-What should I change her diet to?
-Should she now only eat organics?
-I have heard that some shampoos have bad chemicals; would you recommend one we should switch her to?
-Can she still work out and be active?
-Do you recommend any places for the best wigs?

-Once we start chemotherapy, is it better to stay the night in the hospital, should she need assistance with the post-treatment effects?
-She has a dentist appointment next week; should we cancel that?
-What should we do about her schooling?

I know what you're thinking; that's quite the list of scattered thoughts. As you can tell from the list, my mom is quite the worrier; however, this trait has also made her quite the planner. She is always ahead of schedule and thinks *way* in advance about every single detail. She was already thinking about where I should be sleeping the night after I was administered chemo, when we had yet to even hear the doctor's treatment plan. Even thinking about half the questions her brain was consumed with, I knew she did this because of her great love for me. I also knew that making lists was something that calmed my mother's nerves. So rather than tell her that things like my dentist appointment and shampoo might not be the most important issues to worry about at the moment, I watched and held her hand tightly as she continued to jot down every thought that zoomed through her mind.

My dad, on the other hand, was more like me. He sat there calmly with his iPad, playing games and answering work e-mails. If he was anxious about today at all, he did not make it known to us. It was probably for the best, as he knew I looked up to him for comfort, and my mom's level of unease would skyrocket if the most relaxed family member suddenly broke out in a panic.

Finally, after what felt like hours of sitting in uneasiness, a woman who introduced herself as Brandy signaled to us from the back of the room. Allowing Brandy to lead the way as we slowly trailed, we walked through halls of closed doors. Each door we passed had a child's name written on a white board posted on the front. Boy's names were written in bolded bubble letters and girl's names in loopy cursive ones. Eventually Brandy halted in front of a room with *Carly* written on the board.

"Here we are!" she announced cheerfully "Room number five."

As I took a seat on the paper-covered recliner in the middle of the room, my parents sat in the chairs at the side of the room. Going through the basics of what we could expect, Brandy apologized for the wait and kindly welcomed us to the hospital. I just sat there and half-listened as my dad cracked a few jokes I'm sure he had been planning since breakfast, and my mom rattled off a few of her questions from her extensive list. Brandy was gone shortly after we were settled and informed us that Dr. Franklin would be in shortly with all we needed to know.

Once again, we waited in silence until my dad tried to lighten the mood with, "Do you think they will give you crayons to color the paper on the recliner? That could be fun."

I always appreciated his comic relief, especially in times like these, but by the sheer immaturity of his comment, I think my mom was in too much of a panic to spare an empathetic laugh.

The vibration of the hand sanitizer dispenser outside the door sounded, and the door slowly swung open. "Good afternoon, Freels family! My name is Anna Franklin; I will be Carly's doctor through her entire time here at MD Anderson."

She shook all of our hands and then had a seat at her desk across from where I was sitting. I felt as if I were sitting atop a throne, a feeling that I did not particularly like, as I had to look down on everyone else in the room. I wanted so badly just to blend in and let my parents take care of all of this; however, given that I was the patient, I knew it was far from possible.

"Okay, Miss Carly, how's today been going so far?"

"Umm, overwhelming would be the best word to describe it, but I have a good support system with me today. There are just a lot of unknowns about what's to come, I guess."

"Okay, well let me do my best to help ease your nerves. Today we are just going to have a quick discussion about what your schedule is going to look like these next few months. You have a team of doctors who will look specifically at *your* case of cancer and determine exactly what chemo will be most effective and at what doses. After much consideration and reflection on all the options, we have decided to start you with sixteen days of chemotherapy. We want to attack this aggressively, so we have chosen to do four days in a row, followed by a weekend of rest to recover. This calendar will have you finished by mid-July; then we will reevaluate with scans and decide where to go from there. God willing, that will be all the treatment you need, and you can start your senior year cancer-free; however, let's just focus on taking this one day at a time. We have made an appointment for you to get your port put in tomorrow morning, and one or both of your parents will need to go to a training course to learn how to change the bandaging and clean the pipes for you."

Having done this enough times to know that I had millions of questions, Dr. Franklin looked at me to speak up. But I knew that my mom had more to say, so I signaled her to start. After their game of twenty questions, Dr. Franklin glanced back at me. "When do most patients start losing their hair? Should I go ahead and shave my head?" I nervously asked.

"It depends on the patient and the specific combinations of chemotherapy we choose to use."

Noticing my insecurity, she carefully thought about how she worded the rest of her sentence. "I can, however, inform you that you will be losing all of your hair in the combination we have chosen for you. I know this is not ideal, but we truly believe this plan will give us the highest success rate, and your health is of course our priority."

We wrapped up our first meeting of many more to come with a few more questions and then headed toward the elevators for another quiet ride down to the lobby. Today was definitely not the day of forged normalcy I had been hoping for, but as we waited outside the hospital for our car to be brought down, I realized I had a lot to be thankful for. We were blessed to have caught my cancer early enough to have options. Our family was fortunate to live in Houston, the stationing point of many of the nation's most prestigious hospitals, including MD Anderson—a world-renowned cancer hospital—with respected doctors on staff like Dr. Anna Franklin. I was loved by my family unconditionally and was confident that I did not have to battle this on my own. And lastly, I had the Lord on my side; with him, I could not lose.

Chapter 4

A Sign of the Times

At 8:45 a.m., on May 2, it was fifteen minutes until my surgery. Waiting for the anesthesiologist to arrive to put me under, I was anxiously lying on the operating table. I had just been informed that this *port* everyone kept talking about was a series of pipes that would be wired from my heart and come out of my arm, allowing the chemo chemicals to be fed into my system. This little contraption, called a PICC line, would be a permanent part of me until I had completed my treatments; it was yet another red flag to inform strangers I was no longer a normal high school girl. The anesthesiologist arrived and took a seat at the head of the table. He began to talk to me about the procedure he would be following to put me under; however, the only part I remember was the last words he said before I fell asleep.

"Funny thing is, what I am giving you is actually what killed Michael Jackson! But you don't have to worry," he said with an uncomforting chuckle. "I know how to use it better. You'll be awake with a working port before you know it."

Who in their right mind would tell a helpless patient that the drug currently entering his or her system was what killed the legendary pop king? It was too late for me to worry; I was unconscious and dreaming about the last words I had heard. Suddenly, I appeared on the set of *Thriller*, dragging my body around in the zombie-like fashion I had seen in the classic 1983 music video. I dreamed of Michael Jackson moonwalking across the set, with me stumbling and lurching around in the background.

Before the last howl of the song finished, the doctor was waking me up from my hallucinations by saying, "Everything went smoothly, Miss Freels. Careful with your left arm, as the port may be sensitive. When you are ready, slowly stand up, and I will help you back to the waiting room to meet up with your parents. You may be interested in attending the port-cleaning tutorial with the parent who will be helping you with this. It starts in thirty minutes on the third floor."

Knowing that my father tends to have a stronger stomach for such things, I wasn't surprised when he volunteered to help me care for my port weekly. We walked into the classroom set up on the third floor and scanned the room for an empty table. Finding one toward the back of the room, we picked up a packet at the entrance and headed to the vacant seats. Looking around the room, I realized everyone was just as new and confused in this process as we were. My sense of loneliness and idea that no one would understand vanished as we sat in a class of people with nerves similar to our own.

"Good morning, everybody," the instructor opened. "Welcome to the lesson on how to clean your port. Today we will be learning how to prevent infections, change your bandaging, and avoid blocks in the pipes. Hopefully, you brought someone with you with petite, gentle, and steady hands, given how fragile these wires are and how tight some of the areas you are cleaning can be."

Noticing my father's 6'5" stature and observing his large, rough, country working hands, the instructor hesitantly continued.

"However, with some extra focus and practice, any hands will work."

She carefully put on her gloves and used a dummy to demonstrate how to handle each piece of equipment while keeping each object sterile. She cautiously used Q-tips to scrub the skin under the tubes and injected fluids into the spouts to clear any blocked pipes. After twenty minutes of tending to the dummy's port, she placed an identical dummy on every table.

For the first time since my diagnosis, I saw a look of worry in my dad's eyes. He gently lifted up each port line and tenderly cleaned the stitches holding the piping in place. Although his hands were shaking, he would occasionally look up to smile, reassuring me he would go as slowly as he could to guarantee I did not feel any pain in this process. I felt confident I was in the best hands with him, knowing he couldn't stand the thought of inflicting pain on me; however, it was the next part I was uneasy about.

The instructor made her way back around the class, placing a box on our table that read "handle with care".

"These are the shots that you will vaccinate your patient with daily. My recommendation is that you alternate where you are injecting this shot, as it causes sensitivity and leaves a bruise in the area where it goes in. You can use the arm, leg, or stomach. If the injection is causing severe pain to your child, you more than likely do not have the needle in deep enough."

I glanced back at my wide-eyed father who was now holding one of the shots from the box in his leathery hand. I could tell the thought of having to stick me with a two-inch needle every day was bothering him, but of course he used his humor to mask this feeling of uncertainty.

"I can do this!" he assured me. "It's just like playing darts, right? You will stand against the wall, and I will aim and shoot. We got this."

I feared dealing with needles and developing a new bruise on my body every day, but I knew I could trust my dad to do everything in his power to make this necessity easy for me.

When my dad gave me my first shot that night, I recognized that it was hurting him more than it was hurting me. Unsure of how much discomfort the injection would actually cause, I squeezed a pillow as my dad told me a story to distract me from the pinch of the needle. Although it was actually painful, I tried my hardest not to complain or make a face as he stuck my arm with the barb. I continued to engage in the story he was making up and smiled at him to assure him he was doing a good job.

My family was enduring the same amount of shock as I was, and I did not want to make it harder on anyone by complaining. I knew they would change this circumstance in a heartbeat if they had the power to do so. The Lord had blessed me with two wonderful parents and two caring brothers who were heartbroken; the least I could do was silence my grumbles and be grateful for what I had.

Journal Entry
May 2, 2012

Every night, I thank God for two things: the fact that we were able to catch my cancer at such an early stage and for blessing me with the family and friends he placed in my life. The support I have received throughout this process is incredible, and I couldn't have asked for anything more. My brothers have both come in from college to show their love and support, and my parents are doing everything in their power to make this easier for me. Certain friends of mine have quickly drifted away, uneasy with how to handle this situation; however, the ones who have stuck by my side are such a blessing from the Lord.

Chapter 5

Mirror, Mirror on the Wall

Although I had yet to experience my first treatment, I felt it was wise to go ahead and wig shop in order to be prepared for the inevitable. I could deny it all I wanted, but I knew that hair loss would be an unavoidable result of chemotherapy. I was more scared about the moment my first strand of hair fell than I was about any surgery or test result I had received thus far. I understand how crazy that might sound to an outside observer, but the way I saw it, my hair loss was the tragic ending of my once-normal life. Without this wig, strangers on the street, people in the grocery store, and bystanders in shops would instantly know I was not well and would contribute to the constant whispering I had endured in the school halls. There was no hiding it; I had cancer. Finding a wig that mimicked my current hairstyle would be my comfort in this new world of chaos.

I strolled up and down the rows of manikin heads, observing the texture, length, and color of each wig. There were human hair wigs, synthetic wigs, curly wigs, short wigs, blonde wigs, thick wigs. Any wig you could describe to best match your vision was in this store, but something was still discouraging to me.

"If you purchase a synthetic wig," the sales lady warned, "be cautious around stoves or when you are cooking in general, as they could melt. And absolutely no flat irons!"

At first, I thought she was trying to lighten the mood with a joke, but when her comment was not shadowed by a laugh or even a smile, I realized the seriousness of her comment. *Got it*, I thought to myself, *synthetic is now out of the running. Who would want to risk losing their* second head of hair to a kitchen fire? My mom accompanied me on this *adventure*, along with one of my best friends, Mason, and one of my mom's friends who had undergone chemotherapy herself and knew a thing or two about selecting a wig.

"We will find one you love and feel comfortable in," Mrs. Oelfke assured me. "Until then, do not settle. One thing I know is that if you do not feel comfortable in the wig you choose, you won't feel like yourself and won't want to wear it. Just take a deep breath, and we will get you through the day."

I tried on wig after wig, but no matter how closely it resembled my hair, knowing that it wasn't my own made me feel a lack of confidence. I desired a feeling of security and beauty that a girl should be entitled to but saw every wig as a sign of my struggle. Aware of my rapidly decreasing determination to find a wig, I decided to step outside to get some fresh air. I leaned against the outside brick wall and began to call out in prayer.

> *Heavenly Father,*
>
> *I cannot do this alone. I pray that you show up today more than ever and allow me to see myself as your daughter and a creation of the King of Kings. Every girl deals with feelings of self-consciousness and insecurity, but for me, today is an extreme example. Let my eyes and my heart turn to you in times of anxiety and seek you in moments of defeat. Help me believe that I am fearfully and wonderfully made in your image.*

I took a deep, cleansing breath and walked back through the salon doors. Mason came running over to me with reassurances that she was there as my support and wanted to do anything she could to make this process more uplifting. After my brief second alone with God outside, I too was feeling a lot more at peace with the situation. Yes, I would look different from the other girls in my grade, but my baldness would be a sign of the battle I was fighting with the Lord on my side. This difference in looks would eventually become a symbol of the war we had won.

As Mason and I explored the store for a wig parallel to my own locks, we came to the conclusion that some comic relief was long overdue. We snatched the zaniest wigs we could find and brought them back to the vanity mirror where we were stationed. Blue curly, red frizzy, green straight wigs; I sampled the most bizarre of choices to make the actual options seem less foreign to me. Our strategy proved effective as I tried on a dozen wigs. Pulling the strands up and over my existing head of hair, I gazed at my reflection in the mirror.

"It won't appear so *poofed* when you no longer have your own hair underneath it; it will lay flat upon your scalp like your regular hair would," the consultant assured.

In this wig, I didn't feel ashamed to be different. In this wig, I experienced a sense of confidence I had feared would be absent through these next months of my life. This wig mimicked my own hair in volume, length, color, and texture better than I could have ever dreamed. The Lord had once again answered my prayers and diminished my insecurity, while allowing me to see myself through his eyes as a creation of the king.

Journal Entry

May 4, 2012

Although I haven't lost my hair yet, we decided it would be a good idea to go wig shopping in advance so we could find one that most closely matched my own hair. Also, this way, I will be prepared when the time comes to need one. I went wig shopping today with my mom, Mrs. Oelfke (one of my mom's close friends and a former cancer patient), and Mason. At first, it was really discouraging putting on wig after wig, trying to decide which one looked least strange and not feeling like myself in any of them. Thankfully, we finally found one close to what my hair is now and bought it. It was the best decision to bring along a friend, because when Mason saw my frustration and self-consciousness setting in, she brought over some ridiculous looking wigs to try on for fun to cheer me up. Note to self: Always bring along someone who can make you laugh on days you know are going to be hard.

Having a wig ready takes a big burden off, but the hardest part is going to be waiting for my hair to start falling out. I think once the first chunk falls, I am going straight to the hair salon to get it shaved, because watching it fall piece by piece would be tortuous. Of course, I say that now, but I am sure I will never want to make that move. I recently had the port put in my arm, which draws enough attention to the fact that I am sick; a glowing bald head wouldn't exactly help distract from that fact.

You are all together beautiful my darling, there is no flaw in you.
—Song of Songs 4:7 NIV

Chapter 6

Round One: Fight!

Nerves began to set in as my parents and I wandered down the seemingly endless hallway toward the room in which my chemotherapy would be administered. Our morning started early, and the relatively long car ride to MD Anderson was filled with anticipation about the ten hours of chemotherapy my body would soon be receiving. I carried with me a rather crowded bag of things I felt might be beneficial in keeping my mind occupied—movies, a deck of cards, magazines, my prayer journal—anything to distract me from the thoughts and anxiety of the day.

Sitting while awaiting the arrival of our nurse, I prayed for strength in my faith and my body to endure the treatments without harm. I prayed for my family to have peace of mind, trust in the doctors, and faith in the Lord to have a hand over me. Lastly, I prayed for the medics to have clarity and wisdom over my conditions.

Assuring me I was in the best hands, Dr. Franklin entered the room with a team of nurses who, she explained, had been updated in detail about the day's schedule and procedures. She asked if I was ready to begin and reminded me of the importance of staying hydrated through the entire day to eliminate some of the nausea that tags along with treatments. One of the nurses toward the back of the group stood there, accompanied by a stand with a variety of IV bags hanging from the top. Wheeling it my way, he requested my birthdate and medical record number, just as Michelle had warned me. 09 ... 2 ... 2 ... 413. I hesitated my way through, making it obvious it was the first time I had ever had to repeat the numbers aloud.

"Don't worry," the nurse chuckled. "You will have to tell me this number enough times that you will be reciting it in your sleep."

He confirmed my number matched up with those on each bag and began to unscrew my port line to bind with the tube of the first fluid.

"We call this one the red devil. I am sorry this is the first chemo you will experience, as it is one of the toughest to endure. I am not sure if you have heard about this one in particular, but it has often been known to form sores in your mouth that can make it fairly painful to eat. So we recommend frequently rinsing with salt water while you receive it."

He handed me two anti-nausea tablets and instructed me to press the call button if I had any problems. As we watched the first drops of chemo slowly stream down the tube from the bag into my port line, the three of us were left alone in the unflattering yellow tint of light every hospital room seems to generate.

Drop by drop, the red devil made its way into my system. A bitter aftertaste accompanied each drip that navigated down the tube and into my arm, creating a feeling of nausea. I thought to myself *This metal-like taste must be what causes the mouth ulcers the nurse warned me about*. My parents sensed my sick reaction and quickly stepped into the role of distracters. We turned on season one of the show *The Office* to create background noise; we flipped through tabloids to get our celebrity gossip fix; we played game after game of Guess Who, Scrabble, Monopoly—anything to keep my mind off my level of discomfort and my parents' minds off the pain of watching it.

Three hours later, I watched as the final drops of the red devil trickled from the bag to my port, just like the thousands of drops before them. The machine began to obnoxiously beep, alerting the nurse it was time for my second bag to be attached.

"How are we feeling so far?" she questioned in a tone of empathy.

She ran a few tests and then explained that I would now be wired into two bags: one for hydration and the other for my second type of chemo for the day. Every hour on the hour, she would continue to record my weight, blood pressure, and temperature; other than that, I was instructed just to relax. Given my six-foot stature and the pediatric-sized hospital beds, my feet spilled over the edge of the bed, supported only by the table stationed at the end of the mattress.

This particular chemo lacked the dangerous red tint of the first one and seemed to decrease the uneasiness in my stomach. I received the *okay* from the nurse to walk a few laps around the halls, with the contingency that since I was not disconnected from the fluids, I would have to roll my pole alongside me for support.

The day continued, each hour repetitive of the one before. Certain bags caused me to feel as if all I could do was lie silently in bed, listening to the drops run from the bag, wishing time would speed up. Other bags created few side effects and allowed me to be active. Ten elongated hours were finally up, and I was congratulated by the nurses and my parents for successfully completing my first day of chemotherapy.

Tomorrow would be a shorter, six-hour day; however, it still included another round of the red devil and a few others. I was physically, mentally, and emotionally drained from the first day of treatment. Yet my spiritual mentality was flooded to the brim. The Lord had provided everything that I prayed for earlier that morning. Through him, I had remained positive and had the strength to endure those ten hours. The doctors were given clarity and wisdom in their fields to help cure my cancer. My parents maintained peace of mind throughout the day and were my rock in every sense of the word. When I was feeling helpless, they provided me with encouragement and support. When I wanted to sit in silence and pray through my fear, they sat at my side and prayed with me.

I stayed at the hospital that night to get an early start on my treatments the next day. But unfortunately, I experienced little sleep. The next two days proved to be the same as the first. It became a matter of taking it one hour at a time (some easier than others), fully dependent on the Lord for strength and healing.

Carly Freels

Journal Entry
May 8, 2012

I had my first chemo treatment today. I have three this week, and so far, it hasn't been too bad. But I hear it gets worse with each treatment. I am not going to write much tonight, because I am so exhausted and not feeling too great. I just wanted to get a few thoughts down. I am at MD Anderson right now, because it was a long day. So we are staying the night and getting my second treatment in the morning. My mom is staying with me for the night, but my dad was here all day. They have been so supportive of me through all of this, and I know it will continue to stay that way. I love them.

> Honor your father and mother.
> –Ephesians 6:2-3 NIV

Chapter 7

Clearing the Path:
A Father's Perspective

"I'm all in, Lord; I have placed her in your hands."

Those are the words I typed in my iPhone notes as I watched Carly sleep in her hospital bed. She had just finished her chemo treatments, and she was exhausted.

The past couple of weeks had been a blur. As you have learned by now, Carly was a serious volleyball player. We were in Baltimore for a Junior Olympics Qualifier tournament when this journey began. But in hindsight, I know God had been clearing the path long before that.

Claudia was normally the one who traveled with Carly on these midweek trips, but for some reason, when she told me about the Baltimore tournament earlier that year, I said I would take her. I wasn't sure why I so readily volunteered to clear my schedule for this one, but I instinctively did.

We arrived on Thursday and quickly settled in, with hopes of seeing some of the town before dark. I remember the two of us walking down the steep streets in search of a grocery store to buy a case of water for the tournament, which I knew she was sure to consume over the next couple of days. Carly has always had a playful spirit, and I recall the two of us acting goofy as we made our way through town. For some reason when we are together, we care little about how others perceive us.

As we walked, we visited about how important this tournament was. If the team was going to be invited to the Junior Olympics that summer, they had to have a good showing here. The race started early that next morning. If you have never had the opportunity to experience a competitive girls' volleyball event, it is almost impossible to describe. There are literally a hundred volleyball courts set up, generally inside a major convention center. Thousands of girls between the ages of twelve and eighteen are running, laughing, singing, and screaming; it is like nothing you have ever seen. Volleyballs—and I mean hundreds of volleyballs—are flying everywhere as teams warm up and games commence. Parents are equally engaged, most thinking that their little girl is going to be the next Logan Tom or Misty May-Treanor.

The first day went well; they were moving up through their bracket with little opposition. Again, if you have never experienced a competitive event with select teams, it is hard to describe the intensity. These young ladies are good. That evening, we went out to dinner with the team. At this particular tournament, I was one of the only dads who made the trip, so I didn't have the opportunity to hang with the other fathers at mealtime. But that was okay; I was able to learn that the ribbons in their hair are all coordinated and that color *did* matter. Actually, this is one of the things that I love about girls' volleyball: girls can be girls. They can wear ribbons in their hair, sing their silly chants, dance around the floor, and no one cares or thinks they aren't serious about the sport.

That next day, our lives would be changed forever. Carly and I were having breakfast before the second day of the tournament; her long, thick brown hair was pulled back into a ponytail. I remember thinking what a beautiful young woman she was becoming. Her stature, almost six feet, provides her with legs most women would die for and a sleek neck that was radiant. She has always had a beautiful, infectious smile and large, dark (almost black) eyes. I remember looking at her and realizing she was going to go off to college in less than two years. I stared at her in disbelief; where had the time gone?

As the games began, I pulled up a seat courtside. I loved being down close, and I knew Carly didn't care. I didn't make her nervous, and I wanted to see and "whoop" for her "kills" up close. The first game was a win, but I noticed something as I watched her play. It appeared she had a bruise on her neck, the same neck I'd been admiring over breakfast just a couple of hours before. Had she been hit? If so, I had missed it, but I had watched every rally. I called her over between the games and asked, "Did you get hit?"

She looked at me oddly and said no. I asked to see her neck, and when she tilted her head, the dark spot disappeared. What I was seeing was a shadow of something more serious—a lump, slightly larger than the size of my thumb, had formed on her neck. I asked her if it hurt. She replied that she didn't even realize it was there.

Our conversation was cut short by the start of the next game. She ran back out onto the court as I sat wondering what it might be. She had said her throat was soar earlier in the week, but we assumed it was the spring pollen. Maybe her lymph glands were swollen from that? I watched not only the second game but also the *bruise* on her neck for the remainder of the match. The game ended, and with it, a second lump appeared.

Carly and I were sharing a room at the hotel. As she slept, I laid awake making sure I could hear her breathing from across the room. Occasionally I would get up and walk over to make sure the lump was not restricting her breath. As I leaned in close on one cheek, she woke up and said, "What are you doing?" At that point, I felt as if I had taken my role as a concerned parent a little too far. We both laughed.

God is good; he put me exactly where I needed to be, exactly when I needed to be there. I have no doubt that is why I so readily volunteered to take Carly on the trip. That is why I noticed her beautiful neck that very morning.

As I watched Carly sleep during that first night of treatments, I was at peace. The time that had passed between the diagnosis and the start of her treatment had been ordained. God had given me the time to be angry, to reflect, and above all, to let me know that he was in control. I think it is natural for the first reaction to news of a loved one or yourself being diagnosed with a serious illness is to ask why. "Why me?"

I have learned through this experience that God does not *will* these things to happen in our lives. He simply *allows* them to happen to make us stronger and to force us to depend on him. I once heard that God is actually an acronym for gratitude, obedience, and dependence. I have always been grateful and try to be obedient, but I have always struggled with being dependent on anyone—including our maker.

Although it was Carly who was going through this physical trial, our whole family was going through an emotional and spiritual trial. And I can say wholeheartedly we all learned and grew from it. Personally, I had never really reflected on it, but I intuitively knew we serve a loving

Father and that many of the trials of this world are the result of our shortcomings and an attitude of "I can do this on my own." We ignore his wishes, and many of our wounds are self-inflicted through our own choices. We put things in our bodies that were never intended to be put in well-oiled machines, and we wonder why they break down. We breathe things that we were never designed to breathe and wonder why we get ill.

Meeting with Dr. Anna Franklin (Carly's doctor) as we were planning her treatments, I asked about the effects the chemo might have on Carly's fertility. As her father, I was trying to anticipate the next battle she might face. In my mind, I knew we would beat this rap, and I assumed, at some point, she would want to be a mom. Anna looked at Carly and asked, "Do you want to have children?" Carly answered, "Not now, but someday—absolutely."

Dr. Franklin acknowledged this desire and said she had planned to use a form of chemo that helps preserve the eggs. Inasmuch as she had responded so nonchalantly, I asked her if she knew someone who was an expert on the subject. She kindly smiled and said, "Yes. I will get you one of his cards."

She returned with a business card that noted the name of a fertility expert at another hospital and suggested I speak with that physician.

Knowing that time was of the essence (in the short time since we first noticed the lumps, the cancer had already grown to stage two), my concern was if we would have time to harvest some of her eggs for the future. I was rattled. It was a Friday, and we were scheduled to start treatment the following week. Could we delay without causing additional harm? I left her office and frantically dialed the number on the card. The expert was out, and his first opening was not until the end of the following week. I was in a silent panic; I knew Carly loved children and would one day want to be a mother—not for a while but someday.

That Saturday morning, I had to get away. I went to our ranch and planned to spend the entire day on a tractor—my refuge. As I was driving in, I ran into one of my ranch neighbors. She had heard about Carly and expressed her concern and love. She asked if I had spoken to Patrick, one of our other ranch neighbors. I said no and wondered why she had asked; I knew he was a doctor but didn't know anything else. She said he was at MD Anderson and she would tell him to call me. I gave thanks, without really paying much attention to the information I had just received.

As I maneuvered the shredder through the fields, tears rolled down my checks. I cried out to God on behalf of my little girl. My cell phone rang; I didn't recognize the number but turned off the tractor and answered it anyway. It was Patrick, my neighbor, the doctor with MD Anderson. He told me he had heard about Carly and asked if I needed anything. He then told me he was the head of pediatric oncology at MD Anderson and had been out of town last week when we brought Carly to the hospital. He said he had heard she was assigned to Dr. Anna Franklin; she was the right doctor for her, he confirmed. He then asked me if I had any questions. I told him I was concerned about being unable to connect with the fertility expert before chemo resumed the following week.

He asked who gave me the fertility doctor's name and asked me what Anna had said. I explained to him how I had asked Dr. Franklin if she knew a fertility expert with whom I could speak. Patrick laughed. When I asked him why he was laughing, he said because Anna was *the* expert on fertility, not only for pediatrics, but for the entire MD Anderson Hospital system. When I asked why she hadn't told me this, he answered, "She is not a self-proclaimed expert." That is why I have grown to love this woman whom I refer to as *God's hands and feet*.

This confirmed what I thought I already knew; God had prepared our path. We were in the right place with the right doctor. As I turned the tractor back on, I could feel the burden lift off my shoulders. My mind went immediately to the first book of the Bible, Genesis, when Sarah learned that, despite her age, she would bear a son. Why was I worrying about this? If God wanted Carly to have children someday, Carly would have children.

As the night wore on, I reflected on all the things God had done to prepare us for this day. A few months earlier, Carly had informed me that, despite her love for volleyball, she had decided not to play at the college level. Now this was a big deal; she had already received well over a hundred letters from various schools. To have lost this desire was, in my opinion, God's work. He knew that if she still desired to play and the letters quit coming when she was diagnosed (which they did), she would be devastated.

As stated earlier, God put me where I needed to be. If I hadn't been courtside and noticed the inflammation, it might have been weeks or even months before Carly—thinking it was nothing—informed us of the lump. After all, she was an athlete in top physical shape.

God surrounded us with loving friends and family members who truly cared about Carly's well-being. And he provided us the opportunity to be treated at MD Anderson, a world-class cancer hospital, with a pediatric ward where she would be the oldest (not the youngest) patient. What a difference it made going into a waiting room, seeing the young children, and having your heart pour out to them versus being the youngest in the room, wondering why this was happening to you.

As I stated before, it is my absolute belief that God didn't *will* for this to happen to my precious little girl. He simply *allowed* it to happen.

As I told Carly, "If God wanted to spare you this trial, he would have simply removed the growth from your body, and you would never have known you had it. After all, our Creator did create the heavens and the earth."

So why did he *allow* it to happen? Why did he *allow* Jesus, his only Son, to suffer and die on the cross? Because he knows how the story ends.

"I'm all in, Lord; I have placed her in your hands."

Chapter 8

Curl Up and Dye

There I was once again, sitting in Mr. Wichmann's English class, listening to him lecture on the symbols and important metaphors used in the seemingly ancient tale of *The Scarlet Letter*. Despite the fact that I am here writing this book today, English was never my subject of choice in school. So just like any other day, I sat in the very back of the room, twirling my hair between my fingers, and daydreaming about things that seemed to be more important than Hester Prynne and her scandalous reputation in Salem.

Then I noticed something. It was official; the side effects of chemo had set in and taken over my body. As I ran my fingers through the ends of my hair, roughly fifty strands came out. I frantically gathered my hair and whipped it up into a ponytail to attempt to keep the rest intact. But with the yanking of the rubber band on my now-weakening hair, another handful fell.

A few people around me began to notice and react in one of two ways. Knowing this was the start of it all becoming real, some stared with deep looks of sympathy, while others saw it happening and jerked their heads in the opposite direction, hoping I hadn't noticed them watching. Accumulating now close to a hundred strands in my hand, I tried to construct a plan to subtly get to the front of the class to throw away this unhealthy clump of hair I was clinching in my palm without making an uncomfortable scene. I decided it was more awkward for me to sit there, holding the fallen soldiers, than to be seen throwing them away; I hastily raced to the trash can by the door. I made it safely, without any notice. But as I dropped the collection of my own hair into the trash, the teacher glanced over and unintentionally paused at what he saw, causing the rest of the class to take notice as well. A sea of sorrow-filled eyes stared back in my direction as I wiped the strands from my sweaty grip.

"I'm fine!" I said, with an unconvincing smile. "Carry on, Mr. Wichmann. Please."

"Fine."

It's a word so often thrown around, defined as satisfactory, all right, a feeling of wellness; however, for me that day, "fine" acted only as a cover to mask my insecurity. It is best described in one of my favorite movies, *The Italian Job*. F.I.N.E. is actually an acronym standing for Freaked out – Insecure – Neurotic – and Emotional, and today, that couldn't have been truer.

Finally, the dismissal bell rang, and it was time for my favorite subject of the day—lunch. Practically sprinting out of English class, I locked eyes with the *cutest* senior boy to ever walk the halls of this great high school: the tall, dark, handsome star of the basketball team. And he was headed my way!

"Carly!" he yelled from a few lockers down. Was this real? He knew my name? To this day, I couldn't tell you what the following conversation was even about; I was completely lost in those deep blue eyes of his. So distracted by his looks, I also seemed to absentmindedly forget about the horribly uncomfortable situation that had just occurred in English class ten minutes before and began to playfully twirl my ponytail. We all can predict what happened next. Yep, mid-sentence, out came a chunk of my hair and with it a drawn-out silence, followed by him falsely informing me that he "forgot he had to be somewhere." Cue the end of my social life.

In every class I attended, I was forced to make trips to the trash can to dispose of hair accumulating on my desk. I struggled to smile my way through, imagining it was all going to be okay, hoping that people would not notice. I just wanted to help lower the inevitable level of discomfort taking over the classroom. I don't know if my mask of a smile was more about making everyone around me comfortable or about convincing myself that I was okay. But it didn't seem to be accomplishing either task. My insecurity continued to increase with every strand that fell. I eventually gave up trying to continue my everyday schedule and resorted back to the safe haven of Ms. Christie's room. I sat at her desk during the remainder of the school day, admiring her teaching, refraining from touching my hair, and googling Bible verses with any relation to beauty, confidence, and self-image.

Your beauty should not come from outward adornment, such as braided hair and the wearing of gold jewelry and fine clothes. Instead, it should be that of your inner self, the unfading beauty of a gentle and quiet spirit, which is of great worth in God's sight.
–1 Peter 3:3-4 NIV (emphasis added)

Have I not commanded you? Be strong and courageous. Do not be frightened, and do not be dismayed, for the Lord your God is with you wherever you go.
– Joshua 1:9 NIV

These verses shook me that day. Beauty, although so superficially important in the lives of high school girls (as well as so many others), should not be based on worldly possessions or outward appearances. We are called to be courageous disciples for the Lord, and part of that is having courage to overcome the negativity of society.

This lesson carried over when I returned home from school that afternoon. My mother sat on the couch, surrounded by small gifts and a sea of cards.

"People want to know how you are. They want to know how to help and how to pray for us," she informed me. "I know you do not want the extra attention, Carly, but we can never have too many prayers. What do you think about having a blog? You do not have to do the posts; we can have the family update it, but I think it would just be a convenient way to keep everyone who cares updated."

I stood there motionless for a moment, initially offended by the idea of posting our lives on the web for what seemed like the entertainment of others. However, I recalled something our pastor mentioned one Sunday morning about the process of healing. He said, "The only bad pain is wasted pain; the only fruitless stories are the ones that go untold."

The Lord was using my family and me for a reason. Despite the fact that we were still uncertain of that purpose, I knew if this blog could help just one person, all of this suffering was worth it. This was not about me or my family; it was bigger than that.

So that night, my dad published the first post on "The Carly Freels Update" Blogspot page as follows:

Our Baby Girl

As many of you have heard, our baby girl, Carly, was diagnosed with Hodgkin's lymphoma on April 30, 2012. Although I obviously do not understand God's plan, I know he loves Carly dearly and would not forsake her. I do not believe God wills these types of things to happen, but I do believe he allows them to happen to bring us closer to him. I know I have been down on my knees more in the past two weeks than I probably have in the past two years.

Clayton and Kevin were heartbroken when they heard the news and came home for a couple days. They told Carly that God tests the ones he loves the most. Now they are in constant contact with her and keep her laughing. It will be nice to have the boys close by this summer.

Claudia and I sincerely appreciate your prayers, because we know the power of prayer. We are praying humbly and boldly for a miracle that would remove this cup of suffering from her before she even gets started with treatment but have put it in God's almighty hands.

Please pray for strength and courage for Carly; pray that she will be drawn even closer to her maker during this time.

Thanks in advance for your support.

–Brad

Chapter 9

Hair Today, Gone Tomorrow:
A Mother's Point of View

As Carly's mom, I learned during her treatment that some days were bigger than others, and some were better than others. Since Carly was starting to lose her hair in clumps at this point, she decided it was time to shave her head and be done with it. We knew this would be one of those big and probably bad days. Fortunately, my husband, Brad, (Carly's dad) is friends with a wonderful woman named Betty. She owns and operates a small hair salon.

Carly said she felt most comfortable going to this specific salon, knowing she would avoid the possibility of an uncomfortable encounter with her peers. Betty was more than willing to assist. Upon our arrival, she greeted us with a smile and acted as if we were coming in for a routine trim and blow dry. Betty first cut Carly's long hair to a shorter length to donate and then began shaving it all off. The conversations and the air in the room were kept surprisingly upbeat and light. I am not sure if the five other ladies in the salon had been forewarned, but they were lovely and visited as if nothing unusual were occurring.

Carly remained courageous and friendly as she joked around with all the women near her. No tears fell, no drama occurred, and no complaints were made about why this was happening. Once her hair was gone, she was given a scalp massage/wash and we headed back home, just as we had after every other haircut. Betty knew how to make this important day go smoothly, and we will always be thankful to her for that. To quote Carly's cousin, Travis Hook, "Nothing will break her beautiful spirit and Hollywood smile. Bald on her is beautiful."

Betty had also previously styled two wigs for Carly that matched the style of her hair prior to the buzz cut. One was made with real hair, while the other was synthetic. (The debate continues on which type is best.) A friend had also passed down a pink-colored wig for those days when a little comic relief was needed. One specific night, I recall hearing laughter drift down the stairs as Carly and her brother, Kevin, tried on wigs together in her bathroom. Desperate times call for desperate measures, and it was great to hear their laughter throughout the house.

Carly wore her wig for a few weeks, yet she began to feel as if she were doing it more for the comfort of others rather than for her own security. I remember the day Carly first decided to go wigless to school. The Houston heat was sinking in, the wig was hot, and she didn't feel like herself in it. Getting ready for her debut, we found that a little eye makeup and some earrings can go a long way when you're bald. Carly was so relieved that day when she returned from school. She explained to me how she felt like herself again by not hiding under someone else's hair. We assumed everybody at school knew about her situation by this point, but apparently there was a young man in one of her classes who remained in the dark. He approached Carly after giving her strange looks all during class and said, "Wow ... you must have had a wild and crazy weekend!"

We had grown accustomed to bald heads around MD Anderson, but it was interesting to see how others viewed and reacted to Carly's appearance. Most tried to be polite, and sometimes kids handled it better than the adults. Understand that people want to be respectful, and they have the best of intentions. The fact that Carly looked like a healthy seventeen-year-old girl, yet lacked hair, brought confusion to passersby. For example, a stranger once stopped her and asked if she was a competitive swimmer. I assume that baldness would be the world's best, most natural swim cap, but it was humorous comments like this one that caught us off guard. My advice, if you know someone going through this, is to focus on good features—eyes, face, and smile. As a patient, be prepared for insensitive comments and have a response ready.

One of my favorite events to relate happened when a woman approached Carly and asked if she had undergone chemotherapy. Carly said, "Yes, ma'am, for Hodgkin's lymphoma."

The woman explained that she was currently undergoing treatment for breast cancer and was wearing a wig. She complimented Carly, saying that she looked beautiful and asked if it was difficult to go wigless. Carly replied that she highly recommended it, that it was liberating to feel as if you weren't hiding something, and that it was truly a sign of overcoming the battle. The woman said she was inspired by her bravery and would try herself to let go of the wig security blanket. As stated in the movie *My Big Fat Greek Wedding,* "Don't let your past dictate who you are, but let it be part of who you become."

In her typical fashion, Carly never showed us any signs that she was upset or scared. Having her head shaved, especially as a junior in high school, had to be difficult for her, yet Carly didn't see any reason to make this hard on those around her. She knew it was part of the process of getting well and kept marching forward. Carly knew that we, as her family, would back her 110 percent. She was aware of what needed to be done and faced it head-on without complaint. All in all, it was a big day—not a bad day—because of the way Carly handled it. It is said you can tell the true character of a person by how he or she reacts when things are difficult, and Carly was a trooper.

Her strength of character didn't stop with her hair loss. It shined through one morning when we were scheduled to return to MD Anderson for more chemotherapy. Carly awoke that morning, throwing up from her previous treatment; she requested a trash can by her bed. She could see the emotional exhaustion in my eyes, and realized that if we were going to make her appointment, she would have to have the strength and courage to get us there. With the fight she still had in her, Carly got up, got dressed, packed her hospital bag, handed me the car keys, and said, "Let's go, Mom." Off we went to MD Anderson.

Helpful Hints

As the mom of a child with cancer, I would like to share how we chose to handle some situations, with the hope that it may help other moms in similar situations.

—With Carly, the first chemotherapy treatment didn't affect her as much as later treatments, because she was strong and healthy on day one. Get Zofran for nausea, and take it as directed for the first two days of each chemotherapy treatment. Also, if mouth sores are a side effect, use the provided mouthwash regularly. Do not serve favorite foods right before chemotherapy, because your child might get sick and it won't be a favorite anymore.

—If people ask to bring meals for your family, just pick two days of the week that work for you. On a daily basis, it can become a lot to deal with when you're at the hospital and not sure what time you'll return home. Maybe ask a neighbor or close friend to handle the schedule for dinner deliveries. Our friends and neighbors were very generous, gracious, and ready to assist whenever they could. We appreciated all the love and support and were especially grateful for all the delicious meals!

—I made one corner of the dining room her medication station, because Carly had many prescriptions to take on different days of the week. We bought a large calendar and wrote on it which meds needed to be taken on which days and how many times a day, etc. We also turned the guest room into her injection/bandage changing room, so it stayed clean and was more relaxing for her. You might keep a small bucket or trash can around after chemo in case of nausea. Also, leaving out hand sanitizer for company is suggested, as you don't want germs near your patient with such a low immune system.

—Try to keep life as *normal* as possible. We let Carly do things when she felt well and allowed visitors if she was up to seeing them. Feel free to say no gracefully to visitors when timing is bad. Try to allot time to go outside to get some fresh air at least once a day. If you can travel out of town, do it.

—Our hospital pharmacy was typically backed up, so get your order in early—the day before—if possible. If you don't have to use the hospital pharmacy, have the staff there call your local pharmacy for pick-up later.

—For a typical day at MD Anderson, pack a bag containing but not limited to:

- Tylenol
- water/snacks
- hand sanitizer
- pillow
- blanket/sweatshirt
- gum
- chap stick
- tissues
- magazines
- laptop/Netflix
- iPhone
- chargers

Journal Entry
May 26, 2012

It was time to let go. Time to be brave. Time to fully trust in the Lord to bolster my confidence and shave my head. I had held out for as long as I could. But day by day, the strands continually fell, and the bald spots grew in size. I had the wigs ready for use and had invested in every kind of hat imaginable. I decided that my comic relief through this would be to wear a different animal beanie to each chemotherapy treatment; it was a simple way to lighten the mood for everyone involved. Oddly enough, I felt a strong sense of peace as I made this change—something that could have only been the Lord comforting me. I had never imagined this day would come so easily, but with the Lord by my side and my family backing my decision, I knew I could get through it.

Seeing myself in every passing mirror will definitely be something to get used to. So to help with the transition, I posted quotes on my mirror reminding me of the beauty out of which God created me. Baldness is a sign of strength in weakening illness.

> Be strong and bold; have no fear or dread of them because
> it is the Lord your God who goes before you. He will
> be with you; he will not fail you or forsake you.
> —Deuteronomy 31:6-8 NIV

Chapter 10

Brotherly Love

You find out who really cares about you and your family in times of trial. The *convenience* friendships fall back, and the deeply-rooted ones, showing you daily love and support, rise to the challenge. In my battle, I was overwhelmed by the amount of love shared toward my family and the selfless services of our friends and neighbors. However, there is nothing that can come close to the love of your family, and I was beyond blessed by mine.

I have previously expressed how incredibly wonderful my parents have been through all of this, but there are also two remarkable men in my life who never failed to bring a smile to my face in the toughest of times: my brothers. Clayton, 23, and Kevin, 21, at the time of my diagnosis, were just as uneasy with the findings as the rest of us. When they drove home from college that night, the burden from my shoulders seemed to be lifted. They had the natural ability to ease my nerves and turn off my mind to the chaotic world around me.

I specifically remember them coming into my room, giving me a hug, and telling me that God tests the ones he loves the most and that he never gives us something we can't handle. I responded, "I know; I just wish he didn't trust me quite that much."

I knew they would always be willing to talk or pray with me, but their role in my life has always been more one of comic relief, and I couldn't think of a better time for that than the present.

The first day my brothers accompanied me to the doctor's office, Dr. Franklin looked at us and said, "Okay, so I know the parents; who are these two large men accompanying you this week? Bodyguards?"

Knowing my dad's playful sense of humor, he teasingly replied, "Don't worry so much about their names; just think of them as spare parts, should Carly need them."

Having grown up with my dad's good humor, we were fully aware that this was only a joke. Although an unusual way to get a laugh, it is a good example of how our family stood strong as a unit through thick and thin. My brothers would stop at very little to help me.

In the next few weeks, they came home as often as possible to support me and bring laughter into my life, as well as serve as a sense of distraction from reality. Once summer came, it was a huge gift to have them home for a few months.

My brothers have always been extremely protective of me, like most older brothers are, but in times when circumstances are out of their control—like this one— their instincts were to make any positive difference possible. For Clayton, he knew the importance of my friends and wanted to make sure I always felt their support. He is the artistic one of the Freels' clan and decided to apply that talent to making fun T-shirts to give out to my friends at school. This helped me to feel involved, even when my condition restricted me from being with my peers. At first, I'll admit it was a little weird to see people wearing shirts with my name on them, but I soon realized the reason for doing this was simply to remind me that I was truly supported and prayed for.

There was one particular day during my first round of treatments when I received a text from one of my closest friends, Machaela. We knew each other through our dads, but she went to our rival high school in Houston. What was on the other side of that text instantly lifted my spirits. In support of me in my first round of chemotherapy, over fifty people had worn the shirt Clayton had created. Machaela got everyone who sported the shirt together for a picture, which she sent to me for encouragement. As it was not even my own school, there were people in the picture whom I had never personally met. Just knowing there were so many praying for my healing was what got me through that first day of treatments.

I am immensely blessed by the two brothers the Lord gave me, and I cannot even begin to thank them for the joy and love they provided throughout my hardest times.

A friend loves at all times, and a brother is born for adversity.
—Proverbs 17:17 NIV

Chapter 11

His Healing Hands

We had made it to the halfway point! Ideally, we were eight chemos down with eight to go. Today, I had an appointment scheduled at MD Anderson to run progress scans. I had been informed that this round of scanning was simply to note the effects of the treatments with regard to the status of the tumors. I was advised not to be discouraged if the tumors had not shrunk but joyful if they had not multiplied, as that would be a sign of the chemotherapy doing its job and an indication to continue on our current path.

Just like any other checkup day, we rode the elevator up to the seventh floor, checked in with Michelle, did blood work with the always entertaining Tony, and recorded my height and weight with Alice. The rarer item on the agenda (but still not an unfamiliar one) happened as we checked in on the third floor. I was given heated blankets in the waiting room (my favorite part of these days) and instructed to choose my flavor of contrast medium. In preparation for these CT scans, I was not allowed to eat or drink since the previous night, so although these drinks tasted like a watered-down, expired vanilla milkshake, it was nice to have something in my stomach.

Through my experiences, as well as Coach Young's, we came to the conclusion that the very berry flavor was the least disgusting of the options. By consuming this contrast medium, the dye traveled through my bloodstream to create a higher resolution picture of specific parts of the body and allowed any possible tumors to be spotted more clearly.

After finishing the first bottle of contrast, a nurse called my name from the front of the waiting room. I gave my parents a hug, because they were not allowed to come back with me, and headed back to what was essentially a second waiting room. With a smile, the nurse provided me with a pair of scrubs to change into and a second bottle of contrast. As odd as it may sound, I really enjoyed any time that I was back in this second waiting room. We were upgraded from uncomfortable chairs to an individual recliner and given the opportunity of being in a room surrounded by other patients and no other guests. This naturally generated an environment where people from all different walks of life openly discussed their stories of why and how they ended up at MD Anderson. Because everyone essentially had one thing in common, no one felt the need to put on a strong, unshaken façade, creating a sense of vulnerability among complete strangers.

As I lay there in the scanner, listening to the hum of the machine rotating around me and the voice of the technologist coming over the intercom instructing me when to hold my breath and when I could breathe, I prayed. I prayed for the results to come back with proof of shrinking tumors. I prayed for peace of mind and trust in the Lord's will if that was not the outcome. I prayed for wisdom for the doctors to correctly decipher the scans. And lastly, I prayed for my family and me to remain faithful in knowing that I was held and protected by the Lord's hand.

Once again, there we were, waiting. But this time, it was only minutes or maybe even seconds away from the results of the scans. My mom, dad, and I sat in Dr. Franklin's office, anxiously anticipating the verdict. Although we had faith that the Lord had a plan, as stated in Jeremiah 29, it is hard not to generate nerves over knowing if the cancer cells had been multiplying or if the chemical combinations had proven effective in decreasing growth.

The door slowly creaked open as Dr. Franklin walked in. She remained focused on the folder tightly gripped in her hands. Double and triple checking the pages, she spoke the words that, to this day, make me smile every time I replay them in my mind. "You must have a lot of prayers coming your way. The scans from today are negative. We cannot find any signs of the tumors or cancerous cells at all." Our God is a good God.

"She's cancer-free?" my father questioned in a rejoicing tone.

"Yes sir. Cancer-free! She will still need to finish out her last eight days of chemotherapy as a precaution, but we cannot find anything. I have had great success with four rounds but have never seen this after only two," Dr. Franklin exclaimed.

Praising the Lord and thanking him for my restored health, my mother instantly broke into tears. I smiled ear to ear in disbelief at the goodness of our Creator, and my dad kissed Dr. Franklin.

After celebrating my restored health, true to form my next question was about when I could get back into volleyball. I did not have time to waste, realizing that practices would be starting a week after my scheduled final treatment. Realistically, I knew that I would not be able to participate then, seeing as I had suffered muscle atrophy. Every year, we had a big game called *Play for the Cure* against our rival high school to raise money for Coach Young's medical expenses. I was determined to be in good enough condition to return and be part of the starting lineup for that match. I knew it would be a challenge, but what better way to show the power of the Lord's healing than to have my first game back be in honor of Coach Young's ongoing battle with cancer?

I expressed my goal to Dr. Franklin, and although she didn't say it was impossible, she voiced her concern about the pace at which I was attempting to jump back into volleyball. She understood I wanted to move right back into the swing of a normal high school life, participating in the things I loved most. But although my parents and Dr. Franklin wanted that for me too, they warned me of the dangers of overdoing it too soon. They knew the importance of having the chance to play volleyball my senior year but repeatedly encouraged me to pace myself and remain aware of my limits. I was not in the shape or health that I used to be; I understood that. However, the drive in me to compete still existed.

Dr. Franklin recommended a physical therapist who often worked with recovering cancer patients. I was ecstatic at this news and could hardly wait to make an appointment with her. After being so active my whole life, it pained me to sit around, unable to go on a run through the neighborhood or participate in the pick-up matches I knew my friends were planning. These were simple activities to which I had never given thought. But the moment I was incapable of performing them, I realized how much I had taken them for granted. Now, with the continued healing of the Lord to restore my muscles and the help of an expert, I was determined to be a part of that significant game.

> *God is our refuge and strength, a very present help*
> *in trouble; therefore, we will not fear.*
> *- Psalm 46:1-2 NIV*

Journal Entry
June 12, 2012

Cancer-free!

    Today, I went into MD Anderson because I am officially halfway through my sixteen chemo treatments and had to get some scans to check the progress. When Dr. Franklin walked in with the results of my scans, she looked confused, and her eyes were watering. She looked at my parents and me and said, "You must have a lot of prayers coming your way because your scans are negative."

    She went on to say they could no longer find any cancer cells in my neck or chest, and I was now considered cancer-free! She said it was amazing that all the signs of cancer cells were cleared after only eight treatments.

    But we knew that this was the work of the Lord. God is so amazing! The Lord answers prayers, and I have truly been able to witness the power of prayer. I still have to finish my last eight treatments, but it is going to be so much easier knowing I will be finished with chemotherapy by the start of my senior year!

Let all that I am praise the Lord; may I never forget the good things
He does for me, He forgives all my sins and heals my diseases
– Psalm 103:2-3 NLT

Chapter 12

Work Hard, Pray Harder

She introduced herself as Kelly. She would be my guide and staple in the process of getting back in shape for the big game. The day was creeping up, yet my strength was far from ready. Kelly could see in my eyes that I was craving the ability to compete once again, but like everyone else, she warned me of the dangers of pushing myself too hard. My body was weak, and my immune system was even weaker. As much as I hated it, I had to keep that in mind as I strived to better myself physically.

Kelly walked me through a booklet she had prepared for this first appointment. The contents outlined my first month's exercises.

"These are tentative," she explained. "Ideally, we would like to speed up the process, given your very narrow deadline; however, we may also need to delay a few exercises, should your body struggle."

As I flipped through the packet page by page, I felt discouraged at the lack of intensity involved in the listed workouts. It seemed like a workout plan designed for nursing homes. I was used to being challenged and pushed to my very limits in practices. The first two days read as follows:

—Monday
- Water weight: Walk the length of your pool a total of five times. The resistance of the water will help to rebuild your leg muscles. Reminder: do not test these sets; five will be plenty to start off.
- If you are not worn out after the water activity, you may do up to thirty sit-ups.

—Tuesday
- – Bands: Tie one end of your resistance band to a table leg and fasten the opposite end to your ankle. Gauge your exhaustion as you go, but you may do up to ten pulls on each leg, moving away from the table directionally. Attempt to keep the band tight.
- – If you are feeling up to it, you may repeat these motions with your arms. No more than ten pulls per arm.

As I continued reading the outline of my upcoming month, I wondered how these simple exercises would ever get me back into performance shape. I was used to jumping and running sprints. But according to this schedule, we didn't even attempt to test my ability to jump until week two, and that was jumping onto a book. There was to be no running until week three. I was so used to the definition of an *easy* practice as being a mile run warm-up, followed by core strength, volleyball drills, and wrapping up with more cardio. Now, my full workout consisted of nothing but walking to the other side of a pool or moving my leg back and forth ten times. Even then, I was warned to assess my exhaustion after each set in case it was too much for my feeble muscles to endure. It sounded more like a relaxed cool down.

I was determined to complete my appointed workouts to perfection, and I prayed without ceasing for the strength to persevere. I had to accept the fact that I was not the athlete I used to be. Although I took this into consideration, I believed I could build myself back up. With the Lord on my team, there was nothing I could not accomplish; of this I was certain. I would be made strong in the Savior's love.

He gives strength to the weary and increases the power of the weak.
–Isaiah 40:29 NIV

Chapter 13
Chicken Fingers

Did you know that MD Anderson has a personal greeting service? They sure do—my dad. Yes, he took it upon himself to talk to nearly every person who walked through those hospital doors and anyone he passed in the seemingly hallowed halls. I have always known my dad to be friendly to everyone he meets, but during our visits to MD Anderson, his southern hospitality was taken to a whole new level. He realized how blessed we were to have local ties to MD Anderson and saw that many other patients had to travel from other parts of the nation (or world) to receive the prestigious care offered there.

Today's visit was for my third round of chemotherapy. We made the trip to the ninth floor and checked into the inpatient room. Because we had consecutive days of treatment scheduled, we found it easier to stay at the hospital rather than make the journey back to our house for only a few short hours. In addition, the perks of inpatient status included being under the watchful eye of nurses should the side effects of nausea, fatigue, or dizziness take their toll.

My parents and I got situated in our allocated room and made ourselves at home for the long days ahead. We laid out our plethora of movie options, pulled out our box of crafts, and organized our magazine choices. As we say in Texas, this was not our first rodeo. We had found ways to successfully keep my mind occupied while receiving treatments.

Within minutes, our nurse for the day made an appearance. She was a young, perky blonde who introduced herself as Robin. Just like every other nurse, Robin took my weight, blood pressure, and temperature and asked for my medical ID number before wheeling in the IV pole. Something, however, seemed different about Robin; I couldn't put my finger on it, but her zest for life and desire to help differed from the rest.

As the chemo solution fell drop by drop into my port line, I could tell this round would be the cruelest yet. Throughout the process, my immune system grew weaker, making my body more susceptible to the side effects. This was proving true today. My mom called Robin for a bucket as I began to grow nauseous. My body had never felt so vulnerable to the effects of the chemo; yet I had never felt so spiritually or emotionally strong. I knew this feeling was due to the fact that, by the grace of God, my cancer was gone. I understood that this round and the one that would follow it were for precautionary reasons. The finish line was in sight. There's a quote by Thich Nhat Hanh that states, "If we believe that tomorrow will be better, we can bear hardships today." I had faith that even if it was not my literal tomorrow, my future held promises, and the hardships of today would soon be part of my past.

I completed the day's treatment around dinner time. My dad rolled me in my wheelchair down to the cafeteria, making racecar sound effects around each corner. I could always count on him to make me laugh after a difficult day. Coach Young had warned me not to eat any of my favorite foods on treatment days; however, I felt today had been tough enough that I deserved some chicken fingers and French fries. I should have trusted Coach Young's expertise, because I felt more nauseous after that meal than ever before. I can honestly say, for the next year or two, even the sight of chicken fingers made me queasy. A note to anyone going through chemotherapy: No matter how much you crave your favorite meal to cheer you up, eat something else to avoid ruining the taste of your favorite dishes.

Later that evening, the night shift nurse came in to check on me. "Who assisted you earlier with your chemo?" she questioned.

"Robin," my mom replied. "We really liked her."

"Oh, yes. Robin is one of our very best," the nurse responded. "Did she tell you her story?"

It turns out that Robin herself had been a patient of MD Anderson at a very young age. She was diagnosed with cancer in her leg; it had to be amputated as a result. You would have never suspected her to be a victim of this adversity, given her optimistic, selfless attitude and the fact that her prosthesis was hidden underneath her scrubs. She beat cancer and went on to cheer at the University of Texas, where she worked to get her degree in nursing. Now Robin was back to serve others at the hospital that had served her only years before. What an amazing story of hope Robin had; yet she remained humble in knowing that her accomplishments were merely a result of the Lord's restoration. She was an inspiration.

I was typically exhausted after battling the effects tied to treatments. Luckily, our family had the luxury of living next door to a big-hearted, sweet friend and nurse named June. On days like this, she would graciously assist my parents in caring for me. Mrs. June transformed our downstairs guest bedroom into a *relaxation room* where she would play spa music and help administer my daily shots or change and clean my port lines. Her gentle touch and expertise in the medical field was comforting when these practices needed to be performed away from the hospital. She cleared her schedule to do this and made us feel calm and secure about each stage of the process.

After taxing chemo rounds, like this one in particular, it was a blessing to have friends like Mrs. June make our day a little easier.

Chapter 14

No Matter What

I had a one-week gap between my recently-completed round three of chemotherapy and my upcoming and *final* round four treatments, and I knew exactly how I wanted to spend it—at the one, the only Camp Ozark. My schedule had worked itself out perfectly so that my treatment break fell during the session in June, when I had always attended camp. It was fate, and I was determined to get the doctor's approval to go.

After much deliberation between Dr. Franklin, my parents, and me, I was finally given the stamp of approval. Although there were concerns about my weak immunity and surrounding myself with such a large crowd, they understood that being back at Camp Ozark would be a way for me to refuel spiritually and feel a sense of summer normalcy.

I was granted approval to go under one condition. My dad had to come with me to make sure I was keeping up with my medications, as well as administering my daily shots. I was aware that this would not be the two-week-long camp experience I was used to, but I was more than willing to take what I could get. Those three days in Arkansas would undoubtedly be the very best of my summer. My dad was a friend of the Torn family, the owners of Camp Ozark, and they very generously offered their cabin to him during our stay.

That same night, I eagerly packed my bags, belting out the camp cheers and songs I had been raised to know and love. Camp had always been a routine event in my summers, something I looked forward to all year around; however, because of my situation, being able to attend this year just made it that much more special.

Even though I had been going without a wig, I made the decision to wear one during my time at camp. I had grown comfortable, even confident, in my baldness around Houston, but it was different when I was away. At home, everyone knew my circumstances. Even if I wore a wig, it was known that the only thing under it was a bare scalp. At camp, where so many familiar faces would surround me, the odds of all 1,500 people there knowing my situation were slim to none. For once, I wanted to blend in with the crowd. I craved to be seen as just an ordinary camper—not a cancer patient. I wanted to maintain the comfortable, high-energy vibe that was Camp Ozark, and I knew that my hairless head would disrupt that.

For me, my baldness was a sign of the trials I had overcome and the disease I had been cured of by the Lord's healing; to an outsider, however, baldness was automatically associated with sickness and misfortune. For these reasons, I made the conscious decision to sport my wigs the next few days.

That next morning, my dad and I loaded up the car and started our eight-hour trip to the beautiful mountains of Mt. Ida, Arkansas. We started our grand journey by listening to the song we played on the way to every chemo treatment entitled "No Matter What" by Kerrie Roberts. This song spoke of how, when life throws us surprises or trials, we are called to trust and love our God. Faith is trusting in him even when you do not understand his plan, and this song, which spoke of just that, had become our theme song these past few months.

After praising God through that melody we had grown to love, the rest of our car ride (courtesy of my father) was filled with Michael Jackson throwbacks. Even though it was not my ideal choice of music, watching my dad play his air guitar for hours on end never failed to make me laugh.

Five pit stops and hours of Jackson tributes later, there we were, sitting at the Ozark gates. We drove in and parked next to the chow hall, where the laughter of the campers and music from the speakers carried beyond the walls. Overpowered by excitement, I burst out of the car and through the cafeteria doors. Immediately, I heard the voice of Katherine Christie shouting from the front of the room as I was simultaneously engulfed by the hugs of friends I had gone to camp with for years. (A reminder: Katherine is my dear friend who came to her mom's classroom, Ms. Christie, to comfort me the day of my diagnosis.)

After half an hour of overwhelming joy, screams of excitement, and endless embraces, I was shown to my cabin. As I walked up to the screen door, I noticed posters and pictures my friends had displayed on the front of our cabin to welcome me back to camp. I was in awe of the love I was being shown within an hour of entering the camp gates.

I carried on through the day, trying my best to keep up with the fast pace of the camp schedule. I hadn't realized before how quickly we moved from place to place. Everyone ran from point A to point B without ever stopping to breathe. There was seemingly so much to do and never enough hours in a day; it appeared there was simply no time for a break. Seeing my struggle to keep up with the overload of planned activities, Katherine suggested that we take a minute to rest on the store porch. My pride restrained me from outwardly admitting my struggle to keep up, so I was secretly relieved that someone offered to stay back with me.

Katherine has always been someone I could shamelessly voice my thoughts to and a person from whom I sought support and advice. She has never failed to direct me onto the correct path, so for that reason and so many more, I viewed her as a mentor in times when I needed clarity. This was one of those times. Because she had committed to serving the entire summer as a camp counselor, we had only been able to have conversations over the phone. Therefore, the time for us to discuss everything going on at home was long overdue.

Katherine sincerely asked how I was handling everything and what the Lord was teaching me in my times of hardship. I told her that because of the unconditional support of my family, things at home were going as well as one could hope in trials like these. We talked about how, at home, I had overcome my insecurities and learned to accept my baldness as a process of healing. However, being at camp and once again reverting to the wigs had been difficult. I wanted so badly to sidestep the unwanted, unavoidable attention I'd receive if I took off the wig, but the intense heat of the Ozarks, as well as the difficulty of feeling like myself in someone else's hair, made me once again crave that freedom.

"I understand what you mean about the unwanted attention," Katherine assured, "but at the same time, you know everyone here only wants you to feel comfortable. You are just as beautiful without your wig, and if that is how you feel your best, you know we will all be right there next to you supporting that."

Seeing I was still concerned about how others would handle it, Katherine went on to say, "What better night to do it too! You have handled these last few months, while still maintaining your sense of humor. Tonight's theme party is when everyone wears their favorite sports jersey! You could use this as a way to take that theme to the next level. So many NBA players are bald anyway; you'd for sure get *best dressed*," she said with a lighthearted laugh.

That was it! I would use tonight as a way to make the transition from wig to scalp. At the same time, I would ensure that those around me saw I was not sensitive about the subject and keep my good humor in a potentially uncomfortable situation.

That night, I put on my Cavaliers jersey and my Rockets sweatband and prepared myself to exit my cabin door. I can honestly say that the second I stepped out into the open and felt the Mt. Ida breeze on my wigless head, I realized I had truly overcome all insecurities I ever tried to hide with the wig. I knew that even the strangers around me would be able to see the healing power of the Lord simply because, even in my condition, I was able to make it to camp and praise him for his miraculous deeds.

I felt more like myself and acquired more energy that night than I had in months. Just like every other camper there, I spent the next few hours playing games, laughing with my friends, and dancing until it was time to head back to the cabin. Other than a few of the youngest campers asking if all their friends could "poke my scalp," everyone treated me exactly the same as if I had hair as long as Rapunzel. And you cannot blame those eight-year-olds for simply being the curious kids they should be.

I think it is safe to say that my dad enjoyed being at camp just as much as I did. He was always fully prepared to administer aid, should I need it; however, this did not at all hinder him from having the camp experience I believe every kid should have. As I walked around camp with my friends, I would see my dad in the gym participating in pickup basketball games or screaming his way down the waterslides. I definitely was not the only one in the family who needed this vacation.

It is so easy to get wrapped up in focusing total attention on the patient in times like these, but what is often forgotten is how the family as a whole is affected. Those long days I spent in treatments and the sick days that followed, my family was there, too. The break in between my chemotherapies was much-needed, and I think that reverting back to the childlike way of racing down a waterslide was the perfect way for my dad to relieve some of his stress.

My last two days at camp were just as spiritually uplifting as the first. Days filled with encouragement, prayers, and laughter proved to be the best medicine. I drove out of the camp gates feeling more supported and cared for than I could have ever imagined. The Camp Ozark family was exactly what I needed at the time, and I will forever be thankful for the unconditional love I was given there.

Although I realize most cancer patients will not be able to have a camp experience, my recommendation is to find a couple of days to get far away from reality. Find a retreat that makes you happy. You deserve it. If nothing else, just allow some time to get fresh air. Go on a picnic, go fishing, attend a baseball game, or just get outside to feel a sense of renewal. It makes the world of difference in how you feel physically and mentally.

I knew that this fourth and final round of chemotherapy would be one of the hardest physically, but because of the time I had just spent at camp, I had never felt so emotionally and spiritually ready to take on a treatment. With the Lord's help, this was the final push to a clean bill of health, and I was so ready for the day when I could say that, through him, I was healed.

Journal Entry
June 5, 2012

I am at my favorite place in the world right now—Camp Ozark! I had a gap in my chemotherapy schedule so that I could make it up to camp; my dad graciously drove me up to stay for a few nights. I can't even begin to describe how happy I am to be here right now. I have been wearing a wig around most of the week, but tonight, I finally gained the confidence to go wigless. I have been going without a wig when I am with close friends and family, but I had not gone bald around anyone who didn't know my situation. That all changed tonight.

My wig kept sliding off because of the sweat generating underneath it in this Arkansas heat. It was more embarrassing to have to deal with re-taping it to my head than it would've been to reveal myself as bald to such a large group of people.

After talking to Katherine about it and receiving a pep talk from Maggie, I realized everyone at Ozark would be supportive. I have nothing to be ashamed of.

My baldness is a sign of the trials I have overcome, and even more, it is a sign of the miracles God has performed in my life. I can honestly say that tonight, when I exited my cabin bald for the first time, it was the best and most rewarding feeling ever. I could feel all the support of my friends around me, and it just felt so freeing.

> I praise you because I am fearfully and wonderfully made;
> your works are wonderful, I know that fully well.
> —Psalm 139:14 NIV

Chapter 15

Saved by the Bell

The best thing I could compare my last four days of chemotherapy to is finals week in high school. I've worked so hard to get to this point, but I almost don't mind how horrible the entire week has been, because once that final bell rings, it is summer. I am free to go run and play with my friends, spend all day lying out in the sun, or fill my body with junk food.

For me, these last days of treatment were my "final exams." I knew full well that they would be hard and they would be physically and emotionally draining. And just like in school, my thoughts would be flooded with how the results would come out. Would I pass the exam? Would I pass the class as a whole, or would I have to repeat it?

As in school, even though I realize the importance of finals and understand that a failed report card would mean that I am not actually done with the course, a part of me does not even want to stress about it. I am close enough to the finish line to see the greatness that lies ahead.

I was anxious of course to see how the test scores would correlate with the effort that I had put in, but I knew the possibility of a free summer was just days away. Outside the hospital doors lay the opportunity for my family and me to have a celebratory vacation to Mexico, and soon I could have the go-ahead from my doctors to start full training to get back into volleyball.

I will save you the details of this final round of chemotherapy and leave it at this. Just like with finals, it was tough. At times, it made me sick, and all my energy was drained. But also similar to finals week, the time was spent in constant prayer for passing scores. With every drop that fell to my IV line, a prayer was whispered.

Even after that final bell rang in school and I was released for the summer, I could never truly clear my thoughts until my final scores were posted. I needed to be informed I was free to move on. My sixteen treatments had been completed; what remained were my final scans—the results to determine if I could move on.

There I was, once again looking at the luminous picture of palm trees in the scanning room, hoping that soon I might be lying under the real thing. Unlike the others, these scans lacked the fear association I often brought to the other exams. No, this time I was filled with peace and clarity in knowing that the Lord was on my side, and there was nothing to be afraid of. Just like many times before, I lay in silence as the scanner passed overhead, instructing me when to breathe and when to remain motionless. Just like all the times before, I spent those quiet hours in constant conversation with the Lord, thanking him for the miracles he had already performed in my life. And just like all the times before, I thought of my family and how, without them, I would not have been able to persevere through so many obstacles.

Finals week was over, and today was the highly-anticipated day the grades would be posted. Although I had always held myself to high standards in school, I had never been so relieved to receive an A+ in my life. According to the doctors, I had passed the final exams with flying colors and was given a complete, clear bill of health.

As a sign of my victory against cancer, I would be given the opportunity to ring the cancer-free bell in the waiting room. Although it may seem silly to be so excited to chime such a simple bell, to me it was the ultimate dismissal bell—one that would release me from a difficult time of testing and ring in the promise that lay ahead.

Journal Entry
July 17, 2012

I had my last chemotherapy treatment today! Although I still feel rather sick from the treatment, it feels awesome to know that I am done and can start training for volleyball. I can have a normal senior year, like all my friends. I get to ring the bell next week after I take my final scans! It is symbolic of conquering chemotherapy and a beacon of hope for the rest of the patients to see the radiating joy of beating cancer.

I have fought a good fight, I have finished the race, I have kept faith.
−2 Timothy 4:7 NIV

Chapter 16

Ring-a-ding-ding,
as Told by Kevin, My Brother

Today was Carl's* day, and she was ready for it. I was honored to accompany her to MD Anderson for her final scan—the scan confirming she is officially, 100 percent cancer-free. It is on this day that she gets to declare her victory over cancer.

Throughout the past few months, Carly had been suffering. I remember coming home from college the day I received the call from my mom that Carly had cancer; I was a wreck. I was terrified to confront her and uncertain about what the future held. But she was not. The first thing she said to me was, "Don't treat me any differently." And so I didn't.

From that day, I never once saw her cry—I never once saw her scared. The only thing that changed was the number of additional Bible verses written on her walls every time I entered her room. While her physical strength took a hit, her mental and spiritual strength skyrocketed. Her attitude was flawless, and she somehow managed to keep a smile everywhere she went. It was at this point that I realized Carly was mature beyond her years, *way* more mature than I.

Because Carly put her faith in God from the beginning, cancer did not shake her. Cancer did not even appear to faze her. Instead, it gave her a challenge. It was an obstacle she knew she could overcome. In time, it began to pull our family together. It pulled our friends together. It not only brought all of us closer to Carly but also to God. Carly, whether she knows it or not, taught me so many things throughout those months. Among *many* other lessons, she taught me what real patience looks like (still working on putting that into action), she showed me what unconditional faith looks like, and she revealed to me what really matters in life. God knew that through Carly's trial others would benefit—and not only me, but hundreds of others. This was God's intention the entire time. He took a young woman, whom he knew would stay strong in her love for him, and used her to glorify him. God has a plan, and no matter what we think or how it may seem at the moment, he knows what is best for us; we just need to let him be in charge.

MD Anderson has a tradition. When someone is declared cancer-free, he or she walks out to the front of the waiting room and rings a bell in front of everyone. It signifies the patient has beaten cancer; it also gives hope to those who are still in the battle. When it was Carly's turn to ring the bell, she had the cutest goofy smile on her face—a smile I will never forget. She walked right up to that bell, waited for permission, and then went to town. I have never seen her so excited. For the first time since the diagnosis, I saw her shed tears—joyful tears. She had officially beaten cancer.

*Carl: the name Clayton and I have been calling her for most of our lives.

Journal Entry
July 24, 2012

Today I got to experience the pure joy of ringing the cancer-free bell at MD Anderson! I have never felt such a burden being lifted from my shoulders as I did when I heard the chime of the bell echoing through the hospital halls. As I repeatedly beat the clapper against the bell walls, the first tear I had allowed my family to witness streamed down my face. It was a tear of pure joy and peace in knowing what I had accomplished through the Lord, our healer. I was simply overwhelmed by his wonders. I am officially done with all things chemotherapy but will never forget the miracles God has performed in my life.

My parents surprised us with a new puppy, and we are leaving tomorrow for a celebratory vacation to Mexico! If you ask me, those two things add up to a pretty great way to celebrate my restored health.

I have told you these things, so that in me you may have peace.
In this world you will have trouble.
But take heart! I have overcome the world.
− John 16:33 NIV

Chapter 17

Ready or Not, Here I Come

Because I only had four weeks in between receiving my clean bill of health and the *Play for the Cure* game, it was crucial to increase my workouts with the physical therapist. Although I had been working with her continually for the past month or so, any bit of progress I made was being reversed in the following round of chemo. I would strengthen my muscles enough to be able to move up in sets, but the side effects of the treatments would instantly take away that hard-earned strength. I was truly starting from square one. I scheduled meetings with the therapist once a week, but on the other six days she provided me with a detailed schedule of workouts I could do on my own.

I was going to do whatever it took to earn back my starting position. I accepted being absent for the end of my junior year, I understood missing out on most of my summer, but I was not going to sit on the sidelines and watch while my senior season of volleyball took place.

The physical therapist, Kelly, helped me to work my way from being able to jog to the end of my driveway to being able to run to the end of my street. Once my legs were strong enough to master that short-distance run, we moved on to jumping. For me, this was the hardest thing to accept and relearn. Having grown up playing volleyball, I didn't understand why I couldn't perform an act that used to be so natural. My once twenty-six-inch vertical had dwindled away to about an inch. Kelly would set a textbook on the ground in front of me and hold on to both my hands for stability. At the start, I could jump onto and step off of the book about five times before needing a break.

Days turned to weeks, but with each minute, I grew stronger. I started each day by completing the workouts Kelly had devised for me and ended each day with an ice bath. Although, in my mind, these workouts seemed like nothing, my muscles did not agree. I wanted so badly to push myself physically to the very limit, but I had to constantly remind myself that after what my body had been through, my muscles grew weary much faster.

Roughly twenty-one ice baths and countless prayers later, I had built up strength to run through my neighborhood and jump rope for a few minutes without needing to stop. Even though I could see I had been making notable progress, I knew I had a much larger distance to go—with only a week to get there. I decided to sit in on our volleyball team's practices to make sure I remembered the drills and the plays we ran in games. I quickly realized that although my achievement of progressing from jumping on a book to jumping rope for five minutes was something to be proud of, having the endurance to play at a varsity level for an hour-long game was a much greater task.

Starting with my fourth and final week before the big game, I decided that, ready or not, I needed to participate in the team practices. The team did not expect me to be back so soon, but in my mind there was no more time to waste. I confidently walked through those gym doors, fully dressed in our practice gear, but with one new addition to the wardrobe. A problem I had encountered in my first post-cancer workout was that I no longer had eyebrows or eyelashes to stop the sweat of my very bald head from running into my eyes. Although I found this problem a bit humorous, it would be an issue if sweat were to block my vision in a volleyball game.

My dad recognized the dilemma and made me a *school-spirited* sweatband online to solve the problem. It was black and red, with a mustang on the front and our school name on the back. This unique fashion statement, as my mom referred to it, would solve the problem of the sweat running directly into my eyes.

As word started to spread that I was back in practices, e-mails began to flood my computer and those of my coach and family. A couple of newscasters and magazine publishers called; they wanted to interview me and write stories about "how I accomplished everything that I did."

My initial reaction was one of frustration. I did not want to be in the spotlight. I hated the extra attention and just wanted to return to a normal life. Initially, I did not understand why any of this needed to be broadcasted or why people would care to know my story. Luckily, these interview requests were sent through my coaches before they reached me. Coach Young came to me one day, saying that she had received an e-mail from a magazine publisher in Houston who wanted to put me on the cover and do a four-page spread on my story. She asked my thoughts about this request.

"I would really rather not. Is that okay?" I asked reluctantly, hoping that she would simply agree and drop the subject

"Carly, I know you aren't a fan of the attention and want this behind you, but consider all the people who would read it. Almost everyone out there is affected by cancer, either directly or indirectly, and I think you have a really beautiful story to tell. If you can give hope or inspiration to one reader out there, wouldn't you say an interview would be worth it? Just consider it; let me know tomorrow," Coach Young advised.

"You're right," I uttered in hesitation. I knew it was the right thing to do, and I trusted Coach Young's opinion on the matter. My uncertainty and apprehension sprang from the idea of being in a direct spotlight, much less on the front cover of a magazine delivered to almost every house in our area.

"I will do it *if* you do it with me. I also do not want the article to be about me or anything that I have *accomplished*. I want it to focus on what the Lord has done *through* me. Nothing that has occurred in these last few months was because of anything I did or didn't do; so if I am going to do these interviews, I want that to be the focal point."

Coach Young responded to two magazines, the local news channel, and the Houston newspaper that day, confirming interview times and photo shoots. The writers agreed to Coach Young doing every interview with me and were happy to hear that I wanted to make sure the stories would be written with the intention of helping others; they were not to be just about Coach Young or me.

Houston pastor, Joel Osteen, once said, "Keep honoring God with your life. Stay in peace. Trust His timing, and God will open doors that no man can shut."

My hope was that, by doing these stories, I would be able to honor God with my life and perhaps give a piece of courage and faith to someone out there struggling with a similar situation. Thanks to Coach Young, I realized the importance of that possibility.

Chapter 18

Perseverance on Full Display, as Told by Clayton, My Brother

Growing up with two older brothers, Carly quickly developed a great level of toughness and competitiveness. I am actually convinced that she is the most competitive person in our family. Carly never shied away from playing catch, shooting a shotgun, or even riding a dirt bike. She never asked for or wanted any special treatment, even though she was the only girl. No matter what she set out to do, Carly wanted to prove that she could hold her own.

So, as she insisted, Kevin and I didn't treat her much differently. Sure, we were her big brothers and would always be protective of her, but this did not keep us from throwing a routine prank or a harmless joke her way. Carly built up a tolerance for these shenanigans and soon recognized that the less bothered she appeared to be by a joke, the more likely we were to grow bored and lose interest in messing with her.

Her mental toughness has only continued to evolve throughout her life and continues to be one of her many strengths. Carly has a distinctive ability to remain calm and at peace in times of heightened uncertainty. This characteristic allows her to serve as a leader and leave a lasting impression on everyone she meets.

Although Kevin and I are the older siblings, you can see why we've looked up to Carly for as long as we can remember. When I first received the news that Carly was diagnosed with cancer, I was devastated and emotionally distraught. I was initially upset with God and couldn't understand how he could allow this to happen to her and not choose me instead. As I continued to digest the news, I was quickly reminded that Carly *is* a stud. If anyone could take Hodgkin's lymphoma head-on and continue to carry herself in a way that glorifies God, it was my little sister. We had complete faith Carly would overcome cancer and be a blessing to countless others in the process.

Carly approached the *Play for the Cure* game with the same drive and focused determination she had displayed during her treatments. As she mentioned, one of the first goals she set after being diagnosed was to play in this game. Now, having been healed and blessed with the opportunity, she was going to exhaust all of her physical energy to prepare and make a lasting impact.

I had recently moved home after graduating from college; this gave me the privilege of witnessing her relentless training. During all available moments throughout the day, Carly was making time to get her rehab repetitions in. It was very apparent how much Coach Young and this game meant to her.

School had just started its fall semester, and there was an unprecedented buzz about this game. Students, teachers, faculty, parents, and family friends packed the house to show their support. I had attended the same high school several years before and had never experienced an atmosphere like this one. Even during the warm-ups, there was a level of energy and focus I had never seen out of Carly or her teammates. This was the annual *Play for the Cure* game, which represents something greater than any player, volleyball program, or school. Oh, and the event was only magnified as Memorial High School was playing its long-term, spirited rival, the Stratford Spartans.

Prior to the teams taking the court, our dad went to half court and delivered a heartfelt message about our family's experience with cancer, our love and appreciation for Coach Young, and our admiration for both schools coming together for such an important cause. He then led the entire gym in prayer. It was an enormously powerful moment for the entire crowd but especially for our family and those close to Carly. What we experienced was a deep cleansing, a conclusion of Carly's illness, and the restoration of a life of normalcy.

As the emotional gym gathered itself, Carly led the Mustangs onto the court like some kind of Athenian warrior princess (less the braids, of course). Her peach fuzz and red sweatband seemed to be doubling as an intimidation tactic. She couldn't have looked more like a fiercer competitor. This was her moment, and she was ready for it.

There was no doubt Stratford had an impressive team that year, but the momentum and energy belonged to the Mustangs that night. Carly was fearless as she owned the front line, coming up with blocks and spikes left and right. Yes, she had lost a step since last fall, but somehow, she willed herself to be in the right place at the right time. Carly helped lead her team to a staggering three-game victory in a best of five series against the school's biggest rival. As the third game was rounding out, chants of "Car-ly Fre-els!" ... "Car-ly Fre-els!" hailed down from the bleachers. Memorial fans initiated it, but it wasn't long until Stratford united in an overwhelming chorus of "Car-ly Fre-els!" ... "Car-ly Fre-els!" ... "Car-ly Fre-els!" God is so good.

To help tell and also prove that I'm not embellishing this story, here is a very sweet letter Carly's coach received from a Stratford player's thoughtful parent the next morning.

Dear Coach Gammill,

I attended last night's annual *Play for the Cure* game against Stratford. My daughter is on Stratford's varsity, so naturally, I was rooting for the Spartans. The outcome of the match did not, however, diminish in any way my absolute amazement at Miss Carly Freels. What a wonderful example of courage, strength, and faith she is! By my husband's rough guess, Carly personally had over ten kills and twenty-five blocks in last night's game. She truly personifies the word *survivor*.

I just wanted you, as her coach, to know she touched many more lives than she could ever imagine with her leadership, confidence, and poise on the court. All the other parents sitting with me were equally in awe.

I could go on and on. I wish Carly all the best this season and as she goes out into the world next year. And I wish Memorial a successful, winning season as well.

Journal Entry
September 4, 2012

Today may have been one of the happiest days of my life. I am officially back in the game of volleyball, and it could not feel better.

My goal through all of this was to get back into volleyball, but a goal without a deadline is only a dream. I was determined to earn my way back into my starting position in the varsity lineup by the Play for the Cure game. And through the healing hands of our Lord and the motivation of my physical therapist, I did just that tonight.

Every year, Memorial and Stratford go head-to-head in a rivalry volleyball game to raise funds for Coach Young's medical bills, as well as show her our endless gratitude for all she has done for our school, despite her deteriorating health.

Every year, the shirts manufactured and sold say "4CY." It's a slogan created to show our support for our coach; however, to my surprise, when the shirts came out this year, the design was different. The front said, "Killing Cancer," with the "I Can" emphasized, and on the back was "One down - One to go. 4CY 4CF"

This week, leading up to the big game, newscasters, magazine publishers, and newspaper editors attended our practices, wanting to interview Coach Young and me together. Because I was not a fan of media attention, I was hesitant when Memorial Buzz magazine asked to put me on the cover and do a full story on me and my "overcoming of adversity." After much prayer and advice from my family, however, I decided the only way I would agree to participate was if Coach Young was featured as well, and we did not focus on me or "my achievements" but on the Lord and his indescribable power. The publishers agreed, and that next month, a four-page spread was released covering the miracles God had performed in my life and those he was continuously performing in Coach Young's.

The game proved to be more than I could have ever imagined. All four stacks of bleachers were packed, and the atmosphere overflowed with cheers of excitement. The Lord's presence was in that gym. Through his strength, I ran out on that court, alongside my teammates, and took victory over our opposing team. No game has ever meant more to me than tonight's game, and I highly doubt any game ever will. Unrelated to anything I did, the Lord provided me with the strength to compete tonight.

Whatever you do, work at it with all your
heart, as if working for The Lord.
— Colossians 3:23 NIV

Chapter 19

Back on Track

As time carried on, my once-routine life began to fall back into place. Being a normal senior student (just as I had hoped to become), I was back in school and participating in daily volleyball practices.

The only thing making me stand out was my lack of hair. My once shiny scalp began to acquire what my dad described as "a five o'clock shadow," and my strength increased with each day. Although I was so excited to be back into the swing of things, it is impossible to go through something of this magnitude and not be forever changed by it. My faith, as well as my family's, had been strengthened beyond words, and I had learned not to sweat the small stuff any longer. Things such as perfection in grades, sports, or even looks no longer consumed my every waking thought. I had learned to seek the Lord for unadulterated satisfaction in life and to be constantly grateful for the blessing of my restored health.

That following year, the Lord gave me much to be thankful for. The cancer experience had provided me with friends to start my senior year—friendships that were Christ-centered. These were friends who stepped up in a time of trouble and selflessly showed me the love of our Lord. I had also been accepted to my dream school, Texas A&M University, and could not wait to start that new and exciting chapter of my life the following fall semester. Furthermore, I was given the absolute honor of being voted homecoming queen for my high school—a title I had never imagined receiving but was thrilled to accept. As I walked out on the football field with the rest of the court, I could only think how this honor had so visibly glorified my God.

Two months later, God provided me with the endurance to run alongside my brothers, Dad, and extended family in the San Antonio half marathon, which my cousin Chelsea had coordinated. This specific race raises money for cancer research through organizations like Leukemia and Lymphoma Society, St. Jude's Children's Research Hospital, and the American Association for Cancer Research. The power of prayer is the only explanation for going from an inability to run to the end of my driveway in June to completing a 13.1–mile course in November.

I continued to see the friendly, familiar faces at MD Anderson with each checkup. Although the gap was progressively lengthened between appointments—from one month to three months to every six months—their warm welcome never waned. It was comforting to make the trip to the hospital without the chemo cloud hovering over my visit and with the certainty that, through God's grace, I was there with the blessing of being in remission.

> O Lord my God, I cried out to you and you healed me.
> –Psalm 30:2 ESV

Chapter 20

"Thy Kingdom Come, Thy Will Be Done"

We do not know God's plan for our lives. The Lord healed me, but others I have known and loved who battled cancer have passed on to heaven.

My grandfather endured 136 chemotherapy treatments but unfortunately passed away ten years after his diagnosis. Although he physically struggled, he continued to live a joyous and fruitful life and was given the opportunity to watch his grandkids grow up. Maybe this was the Lord's plan for him. We were blessed to get to know our grandfather during his time here on earth, and his strength and positivity warmed the hearts of those lucky enough to be around him.

As you also learned through reading my book, one of the most influential people in my life, Coach Young, battled lung cancer for four years. Although she too was challenged daily by her health issues, she never showed fear or uncertainty to her students. She was the strongest person I have ever had the pleasure of calling a friend, and I was beyond blessed to have her as a mentor through my own challenges. Although she passed away when the cancer spread to her brain in 2014, I am reminded daily of the courage she displayed in dealing with adversities. I strive to live my life in bravery, the way she taught me. She will forever be missed but never forgotten.

Life is not always what we want it to be or would have expected, but we are called to trust our Creator and his will. Loved ones may be called home before we believe it is their time, but our God is one of love and justice. He has a plan for each and every one of our lives.

> *Trust in The Lord with all your heart, and lean*
> *not on your own understanding.*
> *—Proverbs 3:5 NIV*

Chapter 21

Shout It from the
Mountaintops: He is Lord.

My hope in writing this book is not to have a best seller, but to demonstrate an opportunity to let the Lord speak through me. If I can provide hope or understanding for one person, I will consider this book to be a success.

I fully believe the Lord can play countless roles in people's lives and answer their prayers in so many ways—if they accept him. Their situations may be different; they do not have to be diagnosed with a serious disease to receive his love.

Here is my personal testimony and belief. The Lord remained my best friend when I felt alone, and he can be your most loyal companion each day. He was my comforter when I felt the need to remain strong in times of trouble, and he can be yours when you simply have a bad day. He acted as my confidence, reminding me I was his creation when I lost my hair. You can rely on him to fill you with confidence when you simply don't like your appearance. He was my strength when I was training to get back in the game of volleyball; he can be yours when there is an obstacle in your way. Lastly, the Lord proved to be my healer against a disease that only he could cure. But you do not need to have cancer to be healed by Christ; he will cleanse your soul. Spiritually, mentally, physically, the Lord is there to heal your scars and restore your well-being.

Because of him and his miracles, I have been healed. What an amazing God we serve.

But thanks be to God who gives us VICTORY in The Lord Jesus Christ.
—1 Corinthians 15:57 NIV (emphasis added)

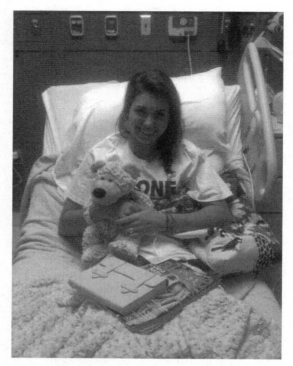

Round one of chemotherapy

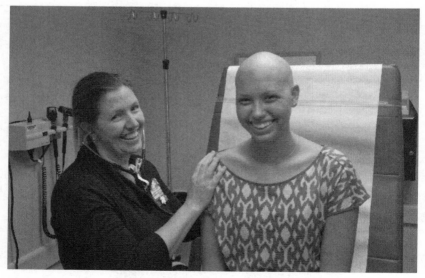

The lovely Dr. Franklin

Supportive friends at Stratford High School

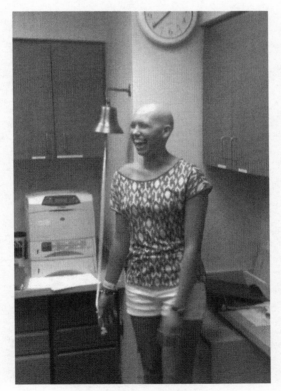

Ringing the cancer-free bell
at MD Anderson

Remission celebration in Mexico
with my wonderful family

Play for the Cure volleyball game
– Coach Young

Being escorted on the field by my dad
at the memorial homecoming game

San Antonio Half Marathon
Our shirts read "No Matter What" (our chosen
theme song through chemo)

"No Matter What"
Lyrics by Kerrie Roberts

I'm runnin' back to Your promises one more time

Lord, that's all I can hold onto

I've got to say this has taken me by surprise

But nothing surprises You

Before a heartache can ever touch my life

It has to go through Your hands

And even though I keep askin' why

I keep askin' why

No matter what, I'm gonna love You

No matter what, I'm gonna need You

I know that You can find a way to keep me from the pain

But if not, if not, I'll trust You

Made in the USA
San Bernardino, CA
07 August 2016